P9-CQS-277

DAVID CUMMING
GEORGE HILLOCK
CLASS 621 87807

T H E
ATLAS of
Endangered
PLACES

☑ Facts On File

FRANKLIN PIERCE
COLLEGE LIBRARY
RINDGE, N.H. 03461

The Atlas of Endangered Places

All rights reserved. No part of this book may be reproduced or utilized in any form or by any means, electronic or mechanical, including photocopying, recording or by any information storage or retrieval systems, without permission in writing from the publisher. For information contact:

Facts on File, Inc.
460 Park Avenue South
New York NY 10016
USA

Library of Congress Cataloging-in-Publication Data

Pollock, Steve (Stephen Thomas)
    The atlas of endangered places / Steve Pollock – Facts on File American ed.
        p.   cm.
    Includes index
    Summary: Text and maps focus on areas of the world in which human activity is destroying the natural balance.
    ISBN 0–8160–2857–5
    1. Man — Influence on nature — Juvenile literature. 2. Man — Influence on nature — Maps — Juvenile literature. 3. Pollution — Juvenile literature. 4. Pollution — Maps — Juvenile literature. [1. Man — Influence on nature. 2. Man — Influence on nature — Maps. 3. Pollution. 4. Pollution — maps] I. Title.
GF75.P65 1993   92-20388
304.2'8 – dc20

Facts on File books are available at special discounts when purchased in bulk quantities for businesses, associations, institutions or sales promotions. Please call our Special Sales Department in New York at 212/683-2244 (dial 800/322-8755 except in NY, AK or HI).

CURR
G
1046
.G3
P6
1993

10 9 8 7 6 5 4 3 2 1

First published in the UK in 1993 by
Belitha Press Limited

Copyright in this format © Belitha Press 1993
Text copyright © Steve Pollock 1993, Illustrations copyright © Belitha Press 1993
Cartography copyright © Creative Cartography 1989
Black and white illustrations by Alan Slingsby, Miniature maps by Eugene Fleury
Edited, designed and typeset by The Book Creation Company, London
Printed in Hong Kong for Imago

Picture acknowledgments: J. Allan Cash 5; Bruce Coleman 13 (bottom: G. Ziesler), 25 (top right: E. and P. Bauer), 48 (top left: B. Wood), 55 (middle left: K. Wothe); Countryside Commission 22; Mark Edwards/Still Pictures 6, 10, 12, 13, 20, 32, 33, 42, 45, 50, 55; Mark Edwards/Biotica 16 (top right: M. Carwardine); Environmental Picture Library (J. Holmes) 42, 45, 46; Geoscience Features 4, 50; Greenpeace Communications Ltd 28 (top right: Greig), 29 (top: Dorreboom); Sonia Halliday 36 (top right: J. Taylor); Robert Harding Picture Library 4, 14, 20, 25, 26, 28, 34 (bottom right: Sassoon), 46 (middle right: Krafft), 54 (bottom right: B. Hawkes), 55 (middle right: M. Claye), 58 (top right: G. Renner); Hutchison 5, 10, 13, 16 (bottom left: B. Regent), 22, 32 (bottom: S. Errington), 36 (top left and bottom: B. Regent), 44, 48 (bottom: F. Greene), 52 (top right: J. G Fuller), 54; Frank Lane 56 (top right: M. Newman); Nature Photographers Ltd 30 (top: H. Miles); Oxford Scientific Films 14 (bottom: S. Morris), 18, 20, 24 (bottom left: R. Villarosa),29, 33, 44 (top: C.P. Allen), 45, 50, 54 (top left: B. Osborne), 56 (bottom left: J. Beatty); Oren Palkovitch 42; Panos Pictures 26 (bottom: H. Bradner), 30 (bottom: K. Burri), 33 (top right: P. Bordes), 34 (top right: D. Reed), 38, 42 (middle right: R.Berriedale-Johnson),44 (middle left: T Bolstad); Rex Features 48 (middle: Ruby); Science Photo Library 10 (top left: Dr G. Feldman), 58 (top left: D. Allan); Frank Spooner Pictures 18, 38 (top left: N. Quido, bottom: G. Merillon), 39 (top left: L. van der Stock, middle right and bottom: G. Bassignao), 40; ZEFA Picture Library 4, 6 (top right and bottom left: W. Williams), 16, 18, 24, 26, 28, 34 (bottom left: Schmied), 46 (top right: Dr H. Kramer), 52 (top left: J. Novak), 58.

CONTENTS

INTRODUCTION

▲ Namibia's Kalahari Bushmen are hunter-gatherers.

Throughout its history, the natural environment, with its mountains, valleys, oceans and rivers, has ceaselessly changed. This natural change usually happens over thousands of years, and no place can ever escape it.

The world has many different types of natural environment, each attracting different kinds of wildlife and each in a natural balance. Rapid change over a short period of time could destroy them or change them so that the animals, plants and people who depend on them can no longer live there. In recent centuries, people have changed their environments very rapidly, putting them at risk.

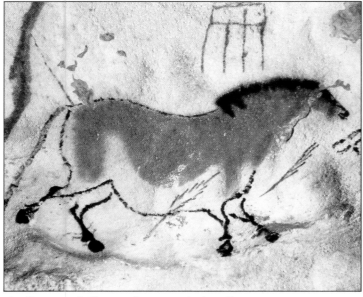

▲ Cave paintings show early hunting scenes.

CONTROLLING THE ENVIRONMENT

The first people needed to control their environment in order to survive. They made tools from flint, and discovered how to make fire with which to cook their food. As people became more advanced, their weapons for hunting improved. Working together in a group, and communicating through language, they began to share these skills. Some of this information was recorded in cave paintings. There is evidence of this form of culture from all over the world, but some of the most famous are in the caves of Lascaux, in

▲ Many ancient woodlands have disappeared.

France. Here, early human artists created images of the animals they hunted, and showed the hunting techniques their fellows used. We know that many of the animals shown in cave paintings have become extinct, not by a natural process, but directly and quite quickly at the hands of these early people. So even in their earliest development, people were able to change their environment to suit their own needs.

▶ If they are not controlled, domestic goats eat all the local vegetation. It is thought that domestic goats were a main cause of the disappearance of the natural Mediterranean forests. Goats, like this Moroccan goat, are still herded, especially in the Third World, and they continue to cause destruction on a huge scale.

◄ A growing population means that more food is needed. One method of supplying more food at a cheaper price is to create enormous fields that can be worked by machines. In Canada, the prairie lands were converted into wheat fields that stretch as far as the eye can see.

THE INDUSTRIAL AGE

With civilization came the need for a range of resources on a large scale. The forests of Europe were cut down, at first for building and fuelwood, then to make way for crops to feed the ever-increasing population. Wood was also needed to build ships for the navies that were to take people to other parts of the world in their search for resources. The woodlands began to shrink, and people turned to a new source of energy – coal.

THE BIRTH OF CIVILIZATION

The ancient hunter-gatherers moved around in search of food – animals for meat, and wild plants, including nuts, berries and roots. They traveled in small groups, because there would not be enough food in one area to feed a large number of people. Hunting and gathering people such as the Kalahari Bushmen live in the same kind of balance with their environment even today.

The situation changed when people began to settle in one place. Once people learned how to grow and store food, and to produce more than they needed at one time, some people became free to stop farming and learn to do other things. Some specialized in building, others drew and painted, and so on, until there were so many different activities going on that civilization was born. Over the centuries, many civilizations have risen and fallen, and each has exploited its environment.

▲ Industrialization changed and polluted the land.

Coal fueled the next stage of civilization, a stage that was to bring the most disastrous changes to the environment. This phase, known as the Industrial Revolution, began in Great Britain, more than 200 years ago. The creation of larger-scale industry called for raw materials, such as the metals dug out of the ground. Factories were built. These polluted the air, the water and the surrounding land with smoke and poisonous waste. In these times, fortunes were made at the expense of the environment and the working people, who sometimes worked in dangerous conditions. Along with industrialization came the need to build cities in which to house the factory workers. Conditions in the cities were terrible, but because the workers had no other method of making a living (they owned no land of their own), they became dependent upon work in factories and mines.

▲ Moscow, a modern industrial city.

THE GROWTH OF INDUSTRY

As industry expanded, the population increased. This growing population needed to be fed. As a result, farming methods became more intensive. The aim was to make each field yield more food. Huge fields were created so that machines could be used for harvesting crops. Chemical fertilizers were introduced to increase yield, and pesticides were used to prevent crops being eaten by insects and other

▲ *Pesticides protect crops but can poison water.*

animals. These practices changed the landscape beyond recognition and poisoned air and water.

Today, pollution is a continuing threat to the environment as a direct result of our industrial way of life. Oil, an essential part of modern existence, is regularly spilt, endangering wildlife and natural places. Other threats include toxic wastes and nuclear pollution.

◀ *Oil is vital to modern life. However, in recent years, oil pollution has destroyed many parts of the environment. The wrecking of the* Exxon Valdez *and the deliberate pollution of the Persian Gulf during the Gulf War, are examples of the devastation spilled oil can cause.*

▲ *New York is an example of a modern city.*

LIVING WITH THE ENVIRONMENT

Throughout history, people have changed their environment to suit their own needs. When people began to use industrial processes, and their population became so large, the environment was threatened. In the process of industrialization, we have created unnatural environments that keep us away from the realities of nature. Living in cities is entirely unnatural, and our day-to-day needs for transport, leisure facilities, food production, waste disposal, energy and industrial production put tremendous strain on the environment in which we live. We have put the existence of our planet and ourselves in danger.

Yet out of this mess there are still places that we value and treasure. There are still the protected areas such as national parks and nature reserves, which we have set aside to flourish as nature intended. Perhaps there are not enough of them, but all over the world there are small havens kept safe from the threats posed by our modern life.

HOW TO USE THIS ATLAS

At the beginning of each entry about a place there are two or three symbols that give information about the place. Each symbol represents a type of change that is taking place in the environment. These changes can have natural causes (for example, the eruption of a volcano), or they can be caused by people (for instance, oil

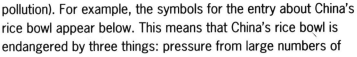

pollution). For example, the symbols for the entry about China's rice bowl appear below. This means that China's rice bowl is endangered by three things: pressure from large numbers of people; changes brought about in agriculture; and soil erosion. The symbols are used on the maps, and you can use them to find out which places are at risk.

THERE ARE 23 SYMBOLS:

 INDUSTRIAL POLLUTION. Places that have been polluted by industry, including air pollution from factories, power stations and motor vehicles. (See p26.)

 FRESHWATER POLLUTION (see pp28-9). Rivers and lakes that have been affected by pollution, including pesticides and fertilizers, acid rain and waste disposal.

 WATER DEMAND. Places that are being put at risk or changed because of increased human need for water. (See Mono Lake, p16.)

 NUCLEAR POLLUTION. Places that are in danger from contamination by radiation from nuclear weapons or power stations. (See p40.)

 WASTE DUMPING. Places where toxic waste, sewage or rubbish have been dumped. (See Love Canal, p16.)

  OIL POLLUTION . Areas that have been contaminated by oil spilled into water supplies or oceans from tankers. (See Oil on Troubled Waters, p38.)

 OIL PIPELINE. Places where leaking pipelines spill oil onto the soil, or create a barrier for migrating wildlife. (See Unnatural Barriers, p18.)

 FLOODING. Places where there is a danger of flooding caused by such things as soil erosion or global warming. (See Global Warming, pp54-5.)

 ACID RAIN. Places that are at risk from acid rain, caused by smoke from industry. (See p20.)

 AGRICULTURE. Environments that have been changed by people in order to grow crops or raise animals. (See p32.)

 TOURISM. Places that are in danger because large numbers of people visit them every year. (See The Mediterranean, p24-5.)

 DAM BUILDING. Areas that have been affected by the building of dams. (See p10.)

 WAR. Regions that have suffered the ill-effects of wars. (See The Vietnam War, p48.)

 CITIES. Places in which vast cities dominate the landscape. (See p22.)

 LARGE POPULATION. Countries threatened by a growing population. (See One-Child Families, p46.)

 POACHING. Regions in which large numbers of animals have been illegally killed. (See p34.)

 DEFORESTATION (see pp44-5). Places in which forests have been cut down. This includes mixed forests that have been destroyed to make way for forests of only one type of tree.

 TROPICAL FOREST DESTRUCTION (see pp12-13). Areas in which tropical forests have been cleared to make way for farming.

 DESERTIFICATION (see pp32-3). Places that are very arid, or are slowly becoming deserts.

 SOIL EROSION (see pp44-5). Places in which people have practiced bad agriculture or reduced the vegetation, leading to soil erosion.

 MINING. Areas that have been changed by mining. (See p10.)

 NATURAL THREATS. Places that are at risk from natural disasters, such as earthquakes, winds and volcanoes. (See Natural Disasters, p46.)

 NATURAL CHANGE. Places that are experiencing a change not directly caused by the actions of people. (See El Nino, p10.)

OTHER FEATURES OF THIS ATLAS
Each large map uses different colors to show different types of landscape and symbols to give you more information about a place:

 Mountain

 Forest and scrub

 Desert

 Arable land

 Frozen desert (snow, ice)

 Game Reserve

 National Park

■ Capital City

☐ Important town or city

▲ Mountain Peak

Each large map has various other features. There is a small locator map, showing where in the world that particular area is. There is also a compass, which tells you where that area is in relation to North, South, East and West. A small ruler tells you the scale of the map - that is, how many kilometers (or miles) one centimeter (or inch) across the map equals. Also, the large maps have lines of latitude and longitude. These are imaginary lines, used to divide the world up into smaller areas, and they are measured in degrees.

7

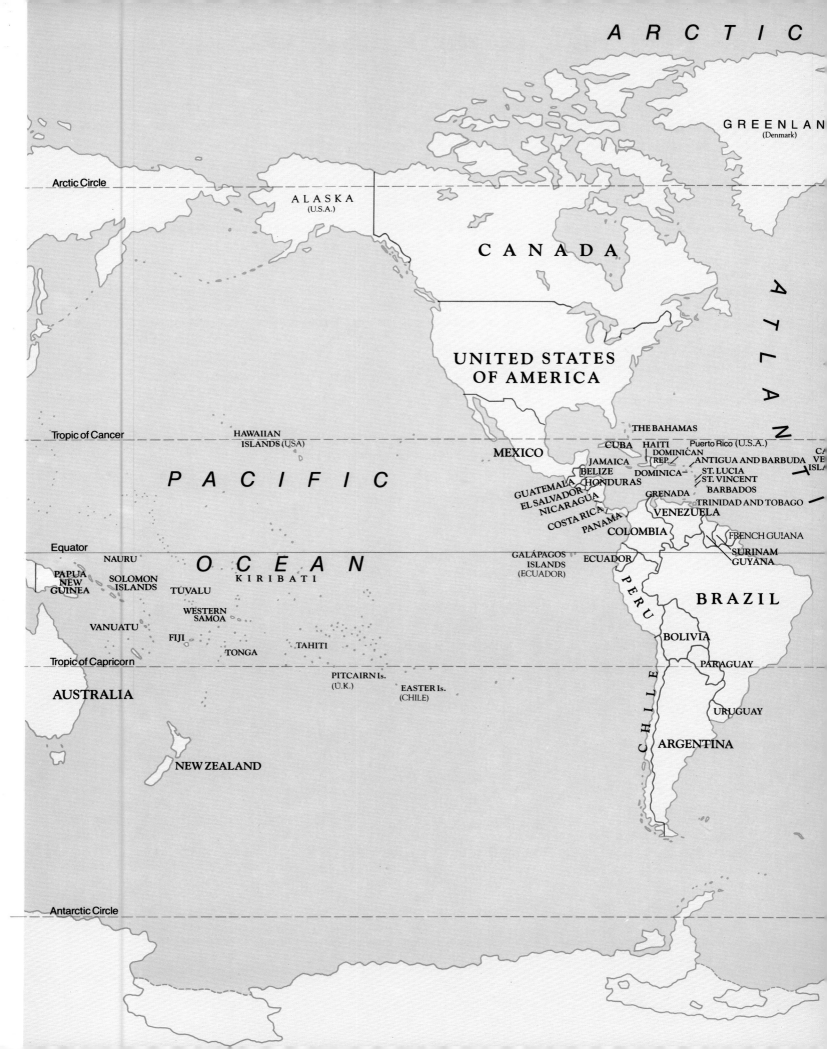

OCEAN

ICELAND

GERMANY
ETHERLANDS
UNITED
KINGDOM
IRELAND

EMBOURG
AUSTRIA
ZERLAND
ANDORRA

PORTUGAL

MOROCCO

STERN
HARA

URITANIA

NEGAL
BIA
NEA-
AU GUINEA
RA LEONE
LIBERIA

NORWAY
SWEDEN
FINLAND

ESTONIA
LATVIA
DENMARK LITHUANIA
BELARUS
POLAND
BELGIUM
UKRAINE
CZECHOSLOVAKIA MOLDOVA
HUNGARY
FRANCE
ROMANIA
ITALY YUGOSLAVIA
BULGARIA GEORGIA
SPAIN
SLOVENIA ALBANIA
CROATIA MALTA GREECE
TUNISIA CYPRUS SYRIA
LEBANON
ISRAEL
JORDAN
ALGERIA LIBYA KUWAIT
EGYPT SAUDI
ARABIA
OMAN

MALI NIGER CHAD
BURKINA
(FASO)
BENIN
TOGO
GHANA
IVORY COAST
NIGERIA
CAMEROON
EQUAT.
GUINEA
GABON
CONGO
CABINDA
(Angola)

THE RUSSIAN FEDERATION

KAZAKHSTAN

UZBEKISTAN

AZERBAIJAN
ARMENIA
TURKMENISTAN
IRAQ
IRAN

TURKEY

KIRGHIZSTAN
TADZHIKISTAN

MONGOLIA

AFGHAN-
ISTAN

CHINA

TIBET

NORTH
KOREA
SOUTH
KOREA

JAPAN

PAKISTAN

NEPAL BHUTAN
BANGLADESH

INDIA

BAHRAIN
QATAR
UNITED ARAB
EMIRATES

YEMEN

SUDAN

DJIBOUTI

CENTRAL
AFRICAN
REPUBLIC

ETHIOPIA

UGANDA
KENYA

ZAIRE RWANDA
BURUNDI
TANZANIA

ANGOLA

ZAMBIA

NAMIBIA
BOTSWANA

ZIMBABWE

MALAWI

MOZAMBIQUE

COMOROS

MADAGASCAR

SOMALIA

MALDIVES

SRI LANKA

SEYCHELLES

MYANMAR
(BURMA)
THAILAND

LAOS

VIETNAM

KAMPUCHEA

MALAYSIA
SINGAPORE

INDONESIA

TAIWAN
HONG KONG (U.K.)

PHILIPPINES

BRUNEI

PACIFIC

OCEAN

PAPUA
NEW
GUINEA

SOLOMON
ISLANDS

INDIAN

MAURITIUS

OCEAN

AUSTRALIA

SWAZILAND
SOUTH AFRICA LESOTHO

OCEAN

ANTARCTICA

SOUTH AMERICA

Three major kinds of landscape make up South America. More than half of it is covered in rainforest, the most precious of nature's wonders. The lifeblood of the forests are the huge rivers of the region, which include the Amazon. A second feature is the Andes mountain chain, which runs down the continent's Pacific side, and contrasts with coastal deserts in Peru and northern Chile. In the north there are tropical grasslands (llanos) and in the south drier grasslands (pampas).

EL NINO ▶

Large numbers of anchovies are caught off the coast of Peru and Ecuador. These fish eat creatures brought to the surface by cold water currents. The satellite picture shows in red the areas where there is most food. Every few years, however, the cold current is replaced by a warm current, called El Nino. The food source then decreases, and so too does the fish population. El Nino is a natural event that has a big effect on the region and elsewhere.

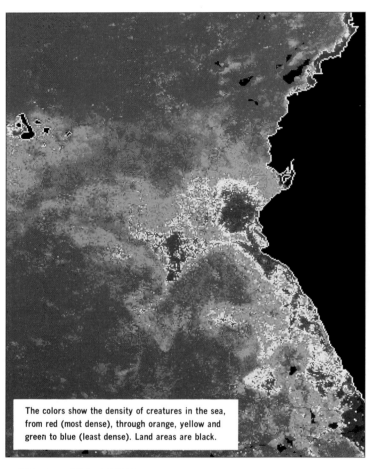

The colors show the density of creatures in the sea, from red (most dense), through orange, yellow and green to blue (least dense). Land areas are black.

MINING ▲

All over the world, people destroy the environment in order to reach the minerals that are found in the ground. In South America, there are vast supplies of bauxite (for aluminium), tin and copper. All these minerals are dug out of the ground, often in forest regions. The forest near mines is quickly destroyed, and waste soil is dumped nearby. This contains poisonous elements, and makes the land sterile.

◀ BUILDING DAMS

Damming rivers in South America has flooded large areas of land, much of it rainforest. In some places, large dams are built across rivers in order to harness their power to provide hydroelectricity for towns and cities. The Guri Dam in Venezuela, for example, provides as much electricity as 10 large nuclear power stations. Hydroelectricity is a clean form of energy, but flooding large areas of rainforest deprives people and wildlife of their homes. In places, dam projects have been canceled, because the cost to the land is too great.

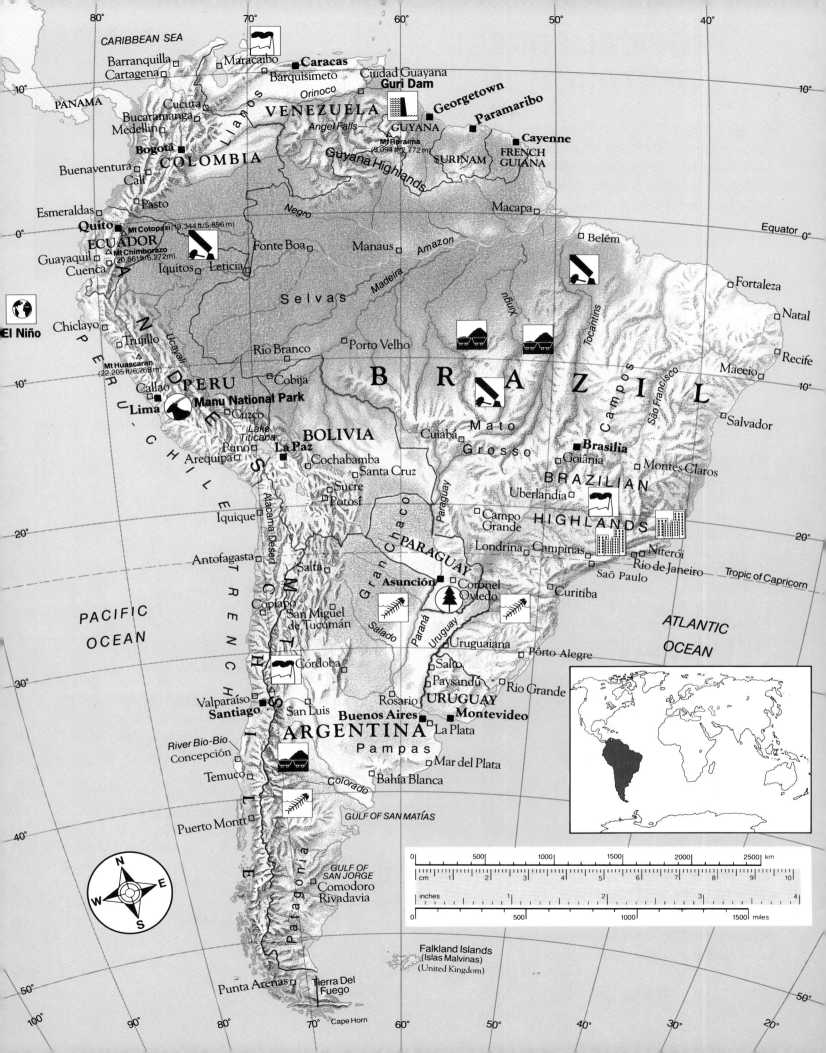

TROPICAL FOREST DESTRUCTION

Tropical forest is the most rich and varied habitat on land. It is an undiscovered treasure house of nature's wonders. Here there are countless different plants and animals, most of which people have never scientifically studied or named.

▶ *In this photograph, part of the Amazonian rainforest is being burned to make way for a large cattle ranch.*

We know that the tropical forests of the world could provide us with many useful resources, yet we are today destroying them at an even faster rate than 10 years ago. Each year we destroy between 16.4 and 20.4 million hectares (40-50 million acres) of forests. This is equivalent to an area twice the size of Austria. If the destruction continues at the same rate, many countries will have removed their entire stock by the year 2035. These countries include Sri Lanka, Haiti, Guatemala and other Central American countries, Thailand, Paraguay, Colombia and Ecuador.

▲ *Huge logging roads are built deep into the forest.*

▶ *This method of rubber tapping is a way of using forest resources without harming the individual trees. This ensures that the resource remains healthy, in order to supply the next generation.*

Most of the world's remaining forest grows in South America. Before people began to destroy it, the South American forest covered 600 million hectares (1.5 billion acres). This is equal to an area two-thirds the size of the USA. The only South American countries in which the tropical forests remain largely untouched, are Guyana, French Guiana and Suriname.

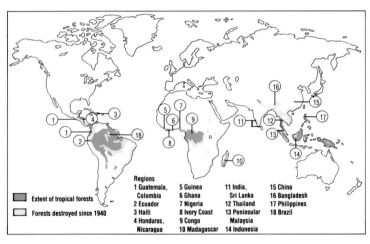

Regions
1 Guatemala, Colombia
2 Ecuador
3 Haiti
4 Honduras, Nicaragua
5 Guinea
6 Ghana
7 Nigeria
8 Ivory Coast
9 Congo
10 Madagascar
11 India, Sri Lanka
12 Thailand
13 Peninsular Malaysia
14 Indonesia
15 China
16 Bangladesh
17 Philippines
18 Brazil

▢ Extent of tropical forests
▢ Forests destroyed since 1940

▲ *This map shows the amount of tropical forest destroyed since 1940. With each passing year the map will change further as more and more of this precious resource disappears.*

REACHING THE TREASURES OF THE FOREST

So how does the complete destruction of these unique places come about? One way is by cutting the forests for timber (logging). The hardwood trees that grow in these forests are very valuable. But many valuable tree species grow only in isolated places that are difficult to reach. It is necessary to build roads into the heart of forests in order to allow machinery and workers to be driven in and the valuable timber to be carried out.

These same roads provide access to the forests for people from overcrowded cities, who are looking for land on which to farm, in order to make a living. These migrants do not know how to use the forest without destroying it. They cut down trees, burn the vegetation and enrich the soil so that they can grow their crops. They grow corn, pumpkins and melons. When the soil tires after about three years, the people move to another area and repeat the destruction.

▲ *Planting fast-growing eucalyptus trees to reduce soil erosion.*

Whole areas of forest are cut down. The wood is sold and the land turned over to grassland. Many large companies build huge ranches on which cattle are reared and sold as cheap meat to many other countries. Without the trees, the tropical rains wash away 185 tons of fertile topsoil from one hectare (450 tons per acre), making the land useless.

FOREST RICHES
Tropical forests contain 155,000 of the 250,000 known plant species. One-fifth of all bird species are found in Amazon forests and 90% of all primates are found only in tropical forest regions of South America, Africa and Asia. Scientists believe that as much as 10% of the world's existing species could be extinct by the year 2000.

▶ *The mahogany tree is very rare, and its wood is valuable. These workers are taking young mahogany trees into the forest to replace trees that have been cut down.*

All these uses of the forest damage it forever. But there are ways to use the forest without damaging it. Rubber trees supply us with the liquid raw materials for making rubber, and they provide a living for people in and around the forests. The forest's fruit trees can also be harvested for food.

Scientists have calculated that one hectare (about 2.5 acres) of untouched Peruvian rainforest could yield fruit and rubber to a value of $6,820. The same area used for cattle has a value of only $2,960 and, when used for timber, is worth $3,184. It is clear that even in economic terms, it is better to preserve rather than destroy rainforests.

MANU NATIONAL PARK

This largely untouched tropical forest in Peru is believed to have the greatest variety of different birds in the world, especially macaws (left). The thick forest is thought to protect the ruins of an ancient civilization, the Paititi. The area has tremendous variety of life and landscape, and ranges from 4,500m (nearly 15,000ft) above sea level in the Andes down to 500m (1650ft) in the basin of the Manu river near the Amazon plains.

CENTRAL AMERICA AND THE CARIBBEAN

The mountains and deserts of northern Mexico give way to more lush tropical forest in the seven other countries of this region. These countries stretch to the south and join up to the continent of South America. In recent years many of these countries have been torn apart by civil war, which has taken its toll not only on the people of the region but also on the natural environment. To the east of this region lie the islands that make up the Caribbean.

HOLIDAY ISLANDS

Some of the Caribbean islands have become a holiday playground of people from all over the world. Other islands have little to offer tourists. These depend on crops to make money. Sugar cane, bananas, cotton, coffee and tobacco are grown on areas of land where tropical forest originally grew. On the island of Barbados the tropical forest was replaced by sugar cane plantations (below).

PANAMA CANAL ▲

The Panama Canal is an artificial waterway that enables ships to cross from the Atlantic to the Pacific oceans. Removal of the tropical forest in some places around the canal has meant that the soil is loose. This soil is beginning to silt up the canal, gradually making it impassable to many larger ships. It is estimated that it will cost millions of dollars to remove the silt. Careless use of the land means that people often have to pay a lot of money to solve problems that need not have arisen if more care had been taken.

▲ Large tracts of land in this region have been cleared so that local people can grow sugar cane.

Today the main industry on the island is tourism. The natural environment of Barbados has been damaged because of pressure put on it by tourists. On the island of St. Lucia (above), however, the tourist industry is smaller and the island has kept most of its forest. The trees act like a sponge, stopping water running away. This ensures that there is water for locals and visitors alike.

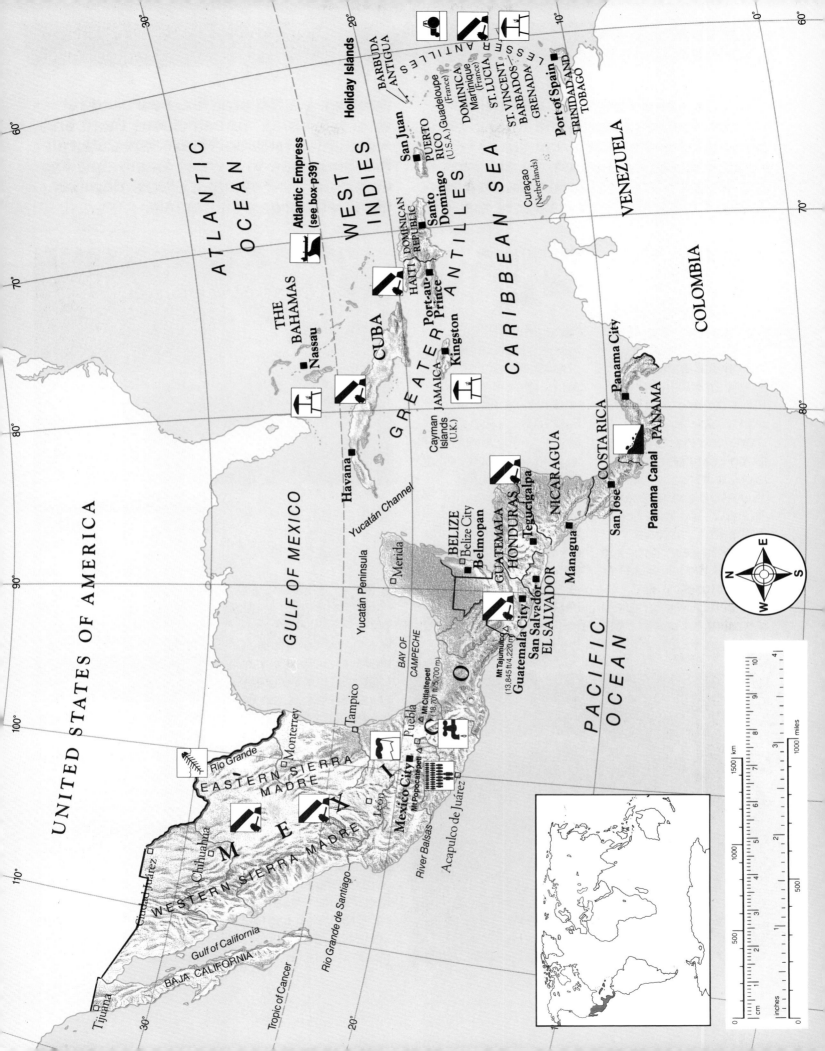

UNITED STATES OF AMERICA

ATLANTIC OCEAN

Tijuana

BAJA CALIFORNIA

Gulf of California

Tropic of Cancer

Ciudad Juárez

Chihuahua

WESTERN SIERRA MADRE

EASTERN SIERRA MADRE

M E X I C O

Rio Grande

Monterrey

Rio Grande de Santiago

León

Mexico City

Mt Popocatépetl

Mt Citlaltepetl
(18,701 ft/5,700 m)

Puebla

River Balsas

Acapulco de Juárez

GULF OF MEXICO

Tampico

BAY OF CAMPECHE

Yucatán Peninsula

Merida

Yucatán Channel

Havana

CUBA

THE BAHAMAS

Nassau

Atlantic Empress
(see box p39)

Holiday Islands

WEST INDIES

San Juan

PUERTO RICO
(U.S.A.)

BARBUDA
ANTIGUA

A N T I L L E S

DOMINICA
Martinique
(France)

Guadeloupe
(France)

ST. LUCIA
ST. VINCENT
BARBADOS
GRENADA

Port of Spain

TRINIDAD AND TOBAGO

VENEZUELA

COLOMBIA

HAITI

DOMINICAN REPUBLIC

Port-au-Prince

Santo Domingo

Curaçao
(Netherlands)

G R E A T E R   A N T I L L E S

JAMAICA

Kingston

Cayman Islands
(U.K.)

CARIBBEAN SEA

BELIZE

Belize City

Belmopan

GUATEMALA

Mt Tajumulco
(13,845 ft/4,220 m)

Guatemala City

San Salvador

EL SALVADOR

HONDURAS

Tegucigalpa

NICARAGUA

Managua

COSTA RICA

San José

PANAMA

Panama City

Panama Canal

PACIFIC OCEAN

1000 miles

500

1000

1500 km

1000 miles

500

cm

inches

The USA has a range of contrasting landscapes. It contains the Rocky Mountains in the west, and the Appalachians in the east. To the west of the Rockies are arid lands and the more fertile California. To the east of the Rockies are the prairies, now used for wheat. Near the Appalachians there are some thick forests. People have altered the landscape to a great extent, building vast cities and planting crops. However, some wild areas still remain.

MONO LAKE ▼

California is a dry state, yet the people who live there need water. The level of the water under the ground, called the water table, lowers as more water is taken. Mono Lake, below, has lost half its water since 1941 to the city of Los Angeles. The level has dropped 15 vertical meters (nearly 50ft), and much of the lake bed is now exposed. This unique lake will be lost forever if the water table continues to fall.

DUSTBOWL ▶

During the 1920s, farmers cultivated the prairies for wheat. Ten years later, they abandoned their huge fields, which they left barren and without plants to hold the soil together. In the 1930s, after several dry years, millions of tons of dry soil blew away. Dust storms (right) are still happening today. In 1977, for example, a dust storm caused 25 million tons of soil to be stripped from the land in 24 hours.

LOVE CANAL ▶

In the early 1940s, a canal was begun in New York City. The project was never completed, however. Instead, a chemical company was given permission to fill the trench with containers full of waste chemicals. Soil was placed over the top of the containers, and the land was then used for building houses. The area became known as Love Canal. In 1978, the people who lived in Love Canal began to move out. Many of them had fallen ill, some were dying. It was discovered

▲ Checking chemical waste.

that the dangerous waste that lay under their houses had leaked out of its containers and was seeping to the surface, causing illness among the residents. Poisonous chemicals are today produced on a huge scale, and their safe disposal continues to be a problem.

CANADA (including Alaska)

The landscapes of the second largest country in the world include frozen wastes in the north, and open prairies where wheat is grown as far as the eye can see in the south. Stretching across the middle, and separating these two very different environments, are dense pine forests dotted with numerous lakes. To the west are the Rocky Mountains, which stretch into Alaska, which is one of the states of the USA, and does not belong to Canada.

OIL SPILL ▶

Canada's natural resources include oil, but transporting oil can be hazardous. In 1989, the tanker *Exxon Valdez* hit a rock and polluted 1,500km (930 miles) of the Alaskan coast with millions of liters of oil.

CLEAR FELLING ▲▶

In parts of Canada the natural forests are clear-felled – every piece of plant material is cut and much of it is churned up by machine into small chips of wood. These are turned into chipboard and other products. This form of forestry leaves ugly scars on the landscape, and it takes a long time for the area to recover. Some forests are replanted with the types of trees that are good for industry. One day, the natural forests will be completely replaced by forests of only a few types of tree.

UNNATURAL BARRIERS ▼

Some oil is transported across Canada by pipeline. When the pipeline was first laid, the caribou, which migrate south in the winter, were stopped in their tracks, unable to cross it. Today the pipeline has been lifted in places to make their passage easier.

18

SCANDINAVIA

Scandinavia, including Norway, Sweden, Denmark, Finland and Iceland, forms the northern part of Europe. Apart from Denmark and Finland, these are all mountainous lands, covered with thick conifer forest. In Sweden and Finland, the forests supply wood and wood pulp for paper which is exported throughout the world. Norway has the characteristic fiords, deep, steep-sided bays which were created by the powerful action of glaciers during the last Ice Age.

ACID RAIN ▶

In recent years, Scandinavia has been affected by acid rain.

This form of pollution is caused by the chemicals in smoke from industry and power stations (below) mixing with rain water. Sulphur, a yellow gas found in this smoke combines with rain water and forms a weak sulphuric acid.

Where this acid rain falls on the land it can weaken trees and other plants. They become diseased and are likely to die in bad weather conditions. Whole forests have died out because of the effects of acid rain.

Much of the air pollution that causes acid rain comes from industrial countries outside Scandinavia. The countries that suffer from acid rain have very little power to stop it.

ACID LAKES AND RIVERS ▼

Acid rain also affects lakes and rivers. It turns the water acid and kills both plant and animal life. Fish cannot use their gills to obtain oxygen in acid water, so they suffocate. Pouring lime into lakes is one way of stopping them becoming completely acid. In the picture above, a helicopter is used to do this. In Sweden, 14,000 lakes like the one below no longer support life.

North Cape
National Park

BARENTS
SEA

Tanafjord

Laksefjord

Varanger Fiord

Lemmenjoki
National Park

Alta

Lake Inari

Tromsø

Nuclear fallout
from Chernobyl
(see p40)

Vesteralen
Islands

Lapland

Narvik

Lofoten
Islands

Kiruna

Mt Kebnekaise
(6,926ft/2,111m)

Bodø

Torne

RUSSIA

Lulea

NORWEGIAN
SEA

Oulu

Skelleftea

Arctic Circle

Umea

Trondheim

FINLAND

Vaasa

Dombas

Mt Glittertind
(8,110ft/2,452m)

Sundsvall

Mt Galdhoppigen
(8,103 ft/2470 m)

Tampere

Lillehammer

Lagen

Glåma

Voss

Bergen

Helsinki

Boknafjord

Turku

Stavanger

Notodden

Oslo

Uppsala

GULF OF FINLAND

Kristiansand

Lake
Vänern

Lake
Mälaren

Stockholm

Skagerrak

Norrköping

Gothenburg

Lake
Vättern

Linköping

Boras

Gotland

Alborg

Kattegat

Oland

Jutland

Arhus

Helsingborg

BALTIC SEA

Esbjerg

Copenhagen

DENMARK

Odense

NORTH
SEA

Bornholm

GERMANY

ICELAND

Vatneyri

Akureyri

REYKJAVIK

Vatnajökull

Hofn

Mt Hekla
(4,747ft/1,491m)

Mt Oraefajokull
(7214 ft/2199 m)

ATLANTIC
OCEAN

0   500 km

cm   1   2   3   4   5   6   7   8   9   10

inches   1   2   3   4

0   400 miles

GULF OF BOTHNIA

N O R W A Y

S W E D E N

The northern parts of West Europe are quite different to those in the south of the region. The cool wet north gives rise to temperate woodlands such as oak. Those countries surrounding the Mediterranean have much warmer climates. The biggest chain of mountains in the region is the Alps ranging across France, Italy, Austria and Switzerland. This region was the first part of the world to suffer from the effects of large-scale industrialization.

HALVERGATE MARSHES ▲

Wetlands are low-lying areas of land that are water-logged. They attract birds, which feed on fish and insects. Water-loving plants also grow here. Halvergate Marshes is a wetland in Britain's Norfolk. As well as being home to plants and animals, it is also the basis of some traditional industries. In 1986, plans were laid to drain the marshes and use the land for crops. Many people protested. They did not want the traditional way of life to disappear and tried to save the marshes' wildlife. In view of the protest, the British government decided that Halvergate should be made an Environmentally Sensitive Area.

The story of Halvergate Marshes is an example of events taking place all over West Europe. In the past, governments encouraged farmers to change the landscape to grow crops. As a result, many original features are disappearing. These include the hedgerows and meadowlands, valuable habitats for wild animals and plants.

Protests against the destruction of wetlands are growing and we may yet save what is left of this natural heritage.

CITIES OF EUROPE ▼

Until the late 1700s in Europe, most people grew crops and lived in villages. Those who did not farm the land earned a living by trading, and they lived in towns. Florence, in Italy (below), is one of these ancient towns. The Industrial Revolution started about 200 years ago in the north of England, and spread rapidly to other northern European countries. Industry brought with it a change in lifestyle for many people. Instead of working the land, many people gathered together around factories, looking for work. As a result, towns and cities grew, roads, shops and houses were built, eating up the green countryside, and, in some cases sprawling into vast agglomerations, such as London, Paris and Frankfurt.

European towns and cities are growing daily, and they are putting more and more pressure on the local landscape. Sewage and industrial waste pollutes nearby rivers, such as the Thames and the Seine. Large numbers of vehicles cause air pollution, and huge by-pass roads make a gash in the countryside.

THE MEDITERRANEAN

▲ *The Costa del Sol, Spain, is a popular resort.*

The Mediterranean is the area of Europe that borders the Mediterranean Sea. It benefits from a much warmer climate than northern European countries, with hot, dry summers and mild, wet winters. For this reason, the Mediterranean has become a tourist destination for one-fifth of the population of Europe.

The Mediterranean coastline is about 48,000km (30,000 miles) long, and 100 million people live in the region all year round. In the three summer months, however, the population doubles in size, swollen by tourists. The governments of the Mediterranean countries have allowed the coast to be transformed, building hotels and other facilities that tourists need. This has brought problems for the local area, including pollution from human sewage and industry, and reduced space for local wildlife.

▲ *Tourists bring mountains of rubbish to the region.*

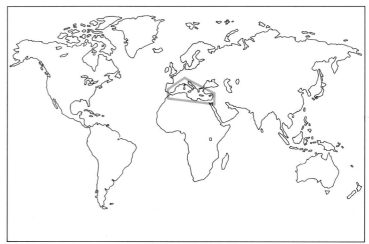

▲ *This map outlines the Mediterranean region.*

▶ *Every year, tons of poisonous waste are discharged by the industries of the Mediterranean region. Waste mercury, for example, has poisoned many shellfish, making them inedible.*

WATER POLLUTION

The disposal of human sewage is always a problem in regions with a high concentration of people. In the Mediterranean region, much of this sewage is allowed to run straight into the sea, most of it untreated. This means that people bathing in the sea risk catching serious diseases, such as typhoid, cholera, dysentery and hepatitis.

The pollution is so bad in some places that beaches have had to be closed. In 1981, a survey showed that one-third of Spanish beaches were below international health standards.

The rivers that empty into the Mediterranean also bring with them dangerous forms of pollution. The River Po, in Italy, flows for 680km (420 miles) before it reaches the sea, and 36% of the Italian population and 20,000 industrial units come into contact with it on its journey. The River Po is responsible for about 80% of the organic pollution of the Adriatic. In 1989, beaches were covered with a green slime that made swimming impossible, and that year, the tourist industry in that region was ruined.

▲ *The natural beauty of Mediterranean islands.*

▲ *The Loggerhead Turtle is disturbed by tourists.*

DISTURBANCES TO WILDLIFE

Visitors create problems for local wildlife. The Loggerhead Turtle, for example, lays its eggs in nests in the sand. The eggs need to incubate for two months, and the temperature of the sand affects the sex of the young. Noise and bright lights from hotels along the shore confuse the turtles and beaches full of sunbathers make a hazardous incubator.

POISONS IN THE MEDITERRANEAN

Some poisonous chemicals dumped in the Mediterranean each year:

Mercury	10 tons
Pesticides	90 tons
Chromium	950 tons
Lead	1,400 tons
Zinc	5,000 tons

There is a great deal of industry on the coast, including oil refineries and chemical factories. Chemical waste from these reaches the sea. The Mediterranean is almost completely enclosed, and so there is little circulation of water. It takes about 70 years for its waters to be renewed. Because of this, pollution remains in the region for a long time.

In 1976, the Mediterranean countries met to sign the Barcelona Convention, a plan to reduce pollution. It was agreed that towns of 10,000 people or more should have sewage treatment systems, and mercury pollution would be cut. If the Convention is honored, there may be hope that the Mediterranean will be cleaned up.

CAMARGUE REGIONAL PARK

This important wetland lies between the estuaries of the Grand and Petit Rhône in France. It is 850 square kilometers (340 square miles) of marshes, freshwater lakes and saltwater lagoons fed by the mud and silt brought down by the rivers. The rivers also bring some pollution, but it remains one of the finest wetland regions in Europe. Wild horses and cattle live here, and it is extremely important for birdlife. Flamingos, waterfowl, waders and many other birds breed here and visit it in the winter.

EAST EUROPE

The most northerly part of this region, Poland, has its coastline on the cold Baltic Sea. At the most southerly point of East Europe lies a warm fertile country, Greece. It was here that ancient Greek civilization blossomed. The region has vast forests and several mountain chains, including the Carpathians and the Balkans. The Danube is the longest river in this region. It flows into the Black Sea, which is surrounded almost completely by land.

INDUSTRIAL POLLUTION

Much of East Europe is industrialized. Shipbuilding, power generation, including

nuclear power plants, mining and chemical works all affect the environment, in the form of land pollution (from dumping waste, for example the slag heap, below left) and air pollution.

Of all the industrialized parts of the world, East Europe has the worst air quality. In Upper Silesia (below), in the southwest of Poland, nearly 3 million people breathe air that has four times the maximum amount of dust allowed by international standards.

Every square kilometer in this region has 1,000 tons of dust created by industry.

Some cities in Hungary, Czechoslovakia and Poland have all recorded levels of sulfur dioxide 10 and sometimes 20 times higher than in the most polluted regions of the USA.

In Hungary, one in 17 deaths is connected with pollution. It is estimated that air pollution in Hungary will cost the country $374 million (about £280 million) in 1990-95, because of illness and early deaths.

However, East and West Europe are now working more closely together, and it is hoped that Western expertise and money will enable East Europeans to reduce air pollution in this region.

DECAYING BUILDINGS

It is not just East European people that are being affected by severe air pollution. In Krakow, Poland, the faces of historic buildings are being eaten away by acidic smogs caused by sulfur pollution (see p20). The ancient and famous buildings of Athens in Greece (above) are being destroyed by air pollution in the same way. More damage has been done to these buildings by industrial and vehicle pollution in the last 25 years, than in the 2,400 years that they have stood.

DENMARK

BALTIC SEA

10°   20°   30°

Rostock

Szczecin

Gdańsk

Oder

Vistula

Bialowieza National Park

Poznań

POLAND

GERMANY

50°   50°

Łódź

Warsaw

Wrocław

ORE MOUNTAINS

Kraków

Prague

CZECHOSLOVAKIA

Ostrava

Brno

Bratislava

CARPATHIAN MOUNTAINS

Košice

Tatra Mountains National Park

AUSTRIA

Danube

Budapest

Miskolc

Debrecen

HUNGARY

Lake Balaton

Hungarian Plain

Cluj

ROMANIA

Szeged

Mureş

Mt Moldoveanul (8,348ft/2,548m)

Braşov

SLOVENIA

Ljubljana

Pécs

Arad

Timişoara

TRANSYLVANIAN ALPS

Ploieşti

Zagreb

Drava

Sava

Danube Delta

Rijeka

CROATIA

Plitvice National Park

BOSNIA

Belgrade

Bucharest

Constanţa

BLACK SEA

ITALY

ADRIATIC SEA

HERZEGOVINA

Sarajevo

YUGOSLAVIA

SERBIA

DINARIC ALPS

Split

D a l m a t i a

Danube

BALKAN MOUNTAINS

Varna

BULGARIA

Dubrovnik

MONTENEGRO

Sofia

Stara Zagora

Burgas

Skopje

Plovdiv

Tirana

MACEDONIA

40°   40°

ALBANIA

Vlorë

Korçë

Mt. Olympus (9,570ft/2,918m)

Thessaloniki

AEGEAN SEA

Lesbos

TURKEY

Corfu

Ionian Islands

PINDUS MOUNTAINS

GREECE

Chios

N W E S

Patrai

Corinth

Athens

Peloponnese

MEDITERRANEAN SEA

Rhodes

0   500 km

cm   1   2   3   4   5   6   7   8   9   10

inches   1   2   3   4

0   500 miles

Crete

30°

FRESHWATER POLLUTION

▶ *This outflow pipe pours sewage into a river in Merseyside, Britain. Sewage provides food for oxygen-breathing bacteria. When populations of such bacteria increase, other forms of river life suffer from reduced supplies of oxygen.*

▲ *The River Danube flows through Budapest, Hungary.*

The River Danube is 2,850km (1,800 miles) long. It starts its life at Donaueschingen, in Germany's Black Forest. Here the water is crystal clear, but as it wends its way through eight different countries in West and East Europe, it changes from a tiny, shallow, clean stream to a huge dirty river, collecting the different pollutants from these countries, on its way to the Black Sea.

THE POLLUTION TRAIL
On its journey, the Danube picks up water from 300 tributaries, but it also collects sediments and pollutants. This process starts as the river passes through the Bavarian Forest, in Germany. It is here

that acid rain (see p20) has weakened and killed many of the trees, leaving the soil free to erode in heavy rains. The soil empties into the Danube and with it go chemical fertilizers and pesticides, starting the first round of pollution. As the river continues, raw sewage from many towns along its bank is added. Industries that use the river water in their industrial processes also pour their waste into it. At just one place, the city of Bratislava in Czechoslovakia, 73 million cubic meters (2,600 million cubic ft) of domestic and industrial waste are dumped into the Danube every year.

Such pollution results in the death of much of the river's flora and fauna. This also leads to the ruination of much of the natural land environment along the way. This pollution process is common to many of the world's rivers. Those countries with large populations and with many industries are the worst.

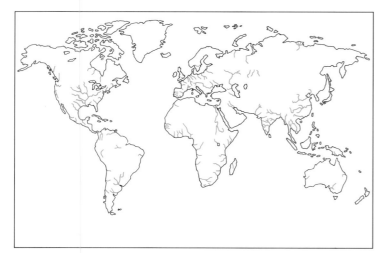

▲ *This map shows the many rivers of the world that are affected by freshwater pollution.*

▲ *The Ganges, in India, is a severely polluted river.*

DEATH OF A RIVER

Nearly all river life breathes oxygen that is dissolved in water. When raw sewage enters the water it becomes food for microscopic bacteria, which rapidly increase in number, using all the river's oxygen, leaving none for other forms of life to breathe, so they either move away to a different part of the river or they die from suffocation.

▲ *Rivers continue to be used for dumping, as this waste plastic in New Zealand's River Kaikorai shows.*

ESTUARY POLLUTION

When a river is badly polluted, the point where it joins the sea is likely to be the worst hit. There are many river estuaries across the world where pollution is particularly severe, and the Danube Delta is no exception to this. The Danube Delta, in Romania, is where the river drops its sediments and its pollutants into the Black Sea. Tulcea, the town at the river mouth, smells of untreated sewage and sulfur. Here, the air is thick with pollutants from an aluminum smelting plant and a power plant. A 1990 press report stated that the Black Sea was turned bright red because of the chemicals poured into it at Tulcea and Sulina.

Such appalling pollution has destroyed much of the wildlife of the Danube Delta. Whole fisheries have disappeared. For example, the sturgeon is a fish on which an entire fishing industry was once based. Because of the pollution of the Danube Delta, the sturgeon population has declined alarmingly. In 1971, local fishermen caught 191 tons of sturgeon, but in 1989, the catch had dwindled, and weighed in at only 19 tons.

DAMAGE TO WILDLIFE

Wildlife such as ducks and geese no longer visit in such large numbers, and the endangered Dalmatian Pelican is down to only 120 pairs.

There is much work to be done if the world's rivers are to be returned to normal. For the Danube, help is at hand, through a major project funded by the World Wide Fund for Nature. With the remaking of East Europe and greater cooperation between all the countries along the Danube's length, there may be a chance that this river will be restored to its full glory.

▶ *The highly endangered Dalmatian Pelican species has to contend not only with pollution of its environment but also the loss of reed beds for nesting and hunting.*

DISASTER IN CALIFORNIA

On Tuesday, July 17, 1991 reports came in of a potential environmental disaster in California. A freight train derailed and a tanker wagon spilled its deadly cargo of 19,500 gallons of weedkiller into the Sacramento River. As the chemicals mixed with the water a poisonous gas was given off, causing at least 100 people in the town of Dunsmuir to be treated for dizziness, breathing problems and nausea. Tens of thousands of fish died and the weedkiller made its way to Lake Shasta, which is a major reservoir for the people of California.

Such accidents happen regularly all over the world. Carrying large quantities of poisons around in this way will put the environment in danger. In this case it was the freshwater environment, but at other times, it has been the air, the sea and the land. As long as people need such chemicals, every place is at risk.

NORTHERN AFRICA

The main landscape of Northern Africa is desert. The huge expanse of the Sahara dominates the region. Many of the countries on the fringe of the Sahara are under threat from desertification, which changes land suitable for growing crops into arid wasteland. In the southwest of the region, the dry desert gives way to savanna and tropical forest. In the northwest lie the great Atlas Mountains. The great rivers of Northern Africa include the Niger and the Nile.

LAKE ICHKEUL ▶

The biggest natural factor creating the most problems for Northern Africa is the constant lack of water.

To make matters worse, supplies of water are being diverted from their sources to supply the needs of cities and farms, and as a result, the water sources are in danger of drying up or of changing so much that the people, animals and plants that once lived there are now unable to do so.

In Tunisia, Lake Ichkeul provides a unique wildlife habitat. The lake is close to the sea, and during the summer, salt water enters the lake and mixes with the fresh water already there. It is this mixing which makes the lake so special. Each winter, the lake is fed by rivers, which ensures that the balance of salt water and fresh water is right.

Now, however, dams are being built across these rivers, cutting off the fresh water supply. Without this water, the lake will turn completely salty, and it will be unable to support wildlife.

◀ THE JONGLEI CANAL

The Sudd is a large area of swampland, fed by the waters of the White Nile. Because it is a wet area in an otherwise dry region, the Sudd attracts a wide variety of animals, plants and people. However, the Jonglei Canal is being built through the swamp to take water for irrigation in Sudan and Egypt. When the canal is completed, a quarter of the water that enters the Sudd will be diverted. Because of this, the Sudd will start to change. It will not be able to support so much wildlife, and one day, it will dry up altogether. The people of the area will no longer have a home, and the people of Sudan and Egypt will have to find another source of water for their crops.

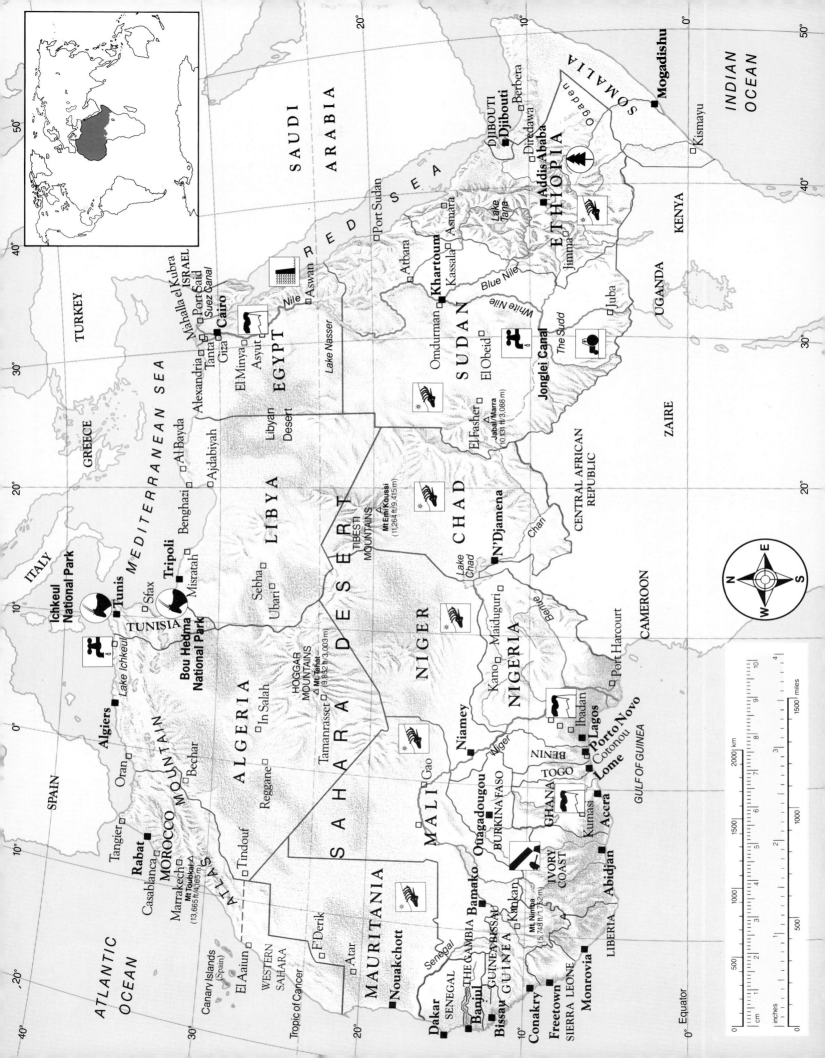

INDIAN
OCEAN

SAUDI
ARABIA

RED SEA

SOMALIA

Mogadishu

Kismayu

DJIBOUTI
Djibouti
Berbera
Diredawa
Addis Ababa
ETHIOPIA
Asmara
Lake Tana
Jimma
Juba

ETHIOPIA

Ogaden

KENYA

UGANDA

Port Sudan

Atbara

Khartoum
Omdurman
Kassala
El Obeid
El Fasher
Jabal Marra
(10,131 ft/3,088 m)

SUDAN

Blue Nile
White Nile
The Sudd
Jonglei Canal

ZAIRE

TURKEY

GREECE

ITALY

MEDITERRANEAN SEA

Suez Canal
Port Said
Mahalla el Kubra
ISRAEL
Tanta
Alexandria
Cairo
Giza
El Minya
Asyut

EGYPT

Nile
Aswan
Lake Nasser
Libyan
Desert

LIBYA

Al Bayda
Benghazi
Ajdabiyah
Misratah
Tripoli
Sfax
Tunis
TUNISIA
Sebha
Ubari

Ichkeul
National Park
Lake Ichkeul
Bou Hedma
National Park

Algiers
Oran
Bechar

MOROCCO

Tangier
Rabat
Casablanca
Marrakech
Mt Toubkal
(13,665 ft/4,165 m)

ATLAS MOUNTAIN

ALGERIA

In Salah
HOGGAR
MOUNTAINS
Mt Tahat
(9,852 ft/3,003 m)
Tamanrasset
Reggane

SAHARA DESERT

TIBESTI
MOUNTAINS
Mt Emi Koussi
(11,264 ft/9,415 m)

CHAD

N'Djamena
Lake Chad
Chari

CENTRAL AFRICAN
REPUBLIC

CAMEROON

SPAIN

ATLANTIC
OCEAN

Canary Islands
(Spain)
El Aaiun

WESTERN
SAHARA

Tropic of Cancer

F'Derik
Atar

MAURITANIA

Nouakchott

Tindouf

MALI

Gao

NIGER

Niamey
Niger

Maiduguri
Kano

NIGERIA

Ouagadougou
BURKINA FASO

Bamako
Kankan
Kanasi
Mt Nimba
(5,748 ft/1,752 m)

THE GAMBIA
Banjul
GUINEA-BISSAU
Bissau
SENEGAL
Dakar
Senegal
Conakry
GUINEA
Freetown
SIERRA LEONE
Monrovia
LIBERIA

IVORY
COAST
Abidjan

GHANA
Kumasi
Accra

TOGO
Lome
BENIN
Porto Novo
Cotonou
Lagos
Ibadan
Ouagadougou

GULF OF GUINEA

Port Harcourt

Benue

Equator

N
E
W
S

0 500 1000 1500 miles
0 500 1000 1500 2000 km
cm
inches

DESERTIFICATION

In Northern Africa, much of the land which once supported local people is turning to desert. In the last 50 years, 65 million hectares of land south of the Sahara have been turned into desert. Desertification is caused by a combination of different factors.

One way to destroy agricultural land is to irrigate it by the wrong method. In hot conditions, water put onto the soil evaporates very quickly. The process of

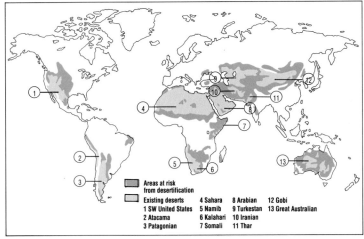

▲ This map shows the deserts of the world, and those areas that could soon turn into desert regions.

▲ These dead trees no longer nourish the soil.

◀ In Burkina Faso, some village women walk for three and a half hours to collect fuelwood for cooking. The trees they cut down are few and far between, and they leave nothing but bare soil behind.

evaporation draws water from underneath to the surface, bringing dissolved salts with it. Many plants cannot grow in soils that contain large amounts of salts. When the water evaporates, the salts remain behind (this is called salination) and make the soil useless for growing crops.

AGRICULTURAL CAUSES OF DESERTIFICATION

In the past, people traveled around this region, taking their animals with them. They moved from one pasture to another, in a journey that ensured that the scarce resources at each location were not used up. Now, however, more and more groups of Africans stay put. They use a small area of grazing land, and their cattle eat everything in sight. When animals are allowed to strip an area of its plants, the natural balance changes and land turns to desert.

More and more African land is now being used to grow cash crops (crops that are not consumed, but which are sold for money). Because of this, people are forced to use poor land, called marginal land, to grow their crops on. This bad quality land quickly becomes useless. If there are other problems, such as soil erosion, salination or drought, it is not long

before a disaster occurs. This is what happened to many of the farmers who live in the Sahel region of Africa, particularly in Ethiopia. The land became a desert and thousands of people starved to death. The lucky ones found their way to refugee camps, where they were provided with food sent by other countries.

▲ Overgrazing by cattle can cause desertification.

◀ *The soil underneath this tree is being held together by its roots. Where there are no roots, the soil has begun to drift away.*

▲ *Sudanese orphans, safe at Itang refugee camp.*

STRIPPING THE LAND

Nearly half of all the people on Earth depend on wood, rather than coal, oil or gas, to cook food and to keep warm. In Africa, the number of trees being cut down for fuelwood is increasing fast. When trees are cut down or when they die because their branches and foliage have been taken, their roots no longer stop the soil from being blown or washed away. When the soil disappears (soil erosion), all that is left is dry, stony soil in which nothing can grow and the land is left to degenerate into wasteland.

However, there is hope for the dry regions of North Africa. In some countries, tree-planting projects have been launched. But it is most important that people are given a chance to own the land they depend on for their food and livelihoods. When they are given this chance, people are more likely to look after their land and adopt better farming practices.

▶ *The ability to dig new wells has encouraged people who usually travel with their cattle to stay in one place. This burdens the water supply and the surrounding vegetation, sometimes leading to desertification.*

LAND UNDER THREAT

UNEP estimates that 3.3 billion hectares (8.15 billion acres) of the world's useful land is at risk of desertification. Every year 6 million hectares (15 million acres) are lost and a further 21 million hectares (52 million acres) become worthless for farming or grazing. By the year 2000, the livelihoods of 1.2 billion people could be at risk.

BOU HEDMA NATIONAL PARK

In 1985, the endangered Scimitar-horned Oryx (left) was reintroduced into the Bou Hedma National Park in Tunisia. In the summer of 1987 the first calf was born. The animals have access to the full protected area of the Park (1,500-2,000 hectares/3,700-5,000 acres), and they are now well-adapted to the habitat, eating the natural vegetation. By reintroducing an animal that used to be common in a region, the natural features that make that place special can be restored.

CENTRAL AND SOUTHERN AFRICA

The most famous feature of the landscape of this part of Africa is its vast rolling grasslands. These are most well known by the name savannas. In the west there are the wet tropical forests. There are also the deserts of the Kalahari and Namib in the south. The most spectacular feature is the great African Rift Valley, a gash in the Earth's surface so deep and long it can be seen from space. This region also includes the unique island of Madagascar.

TOURIST THREAT ▼

Wildlife and scenery attract tourists to Africa's game reserves. Without the tourist industry, local people would be poorer, and could turn to poaching to earn a living. But tourism itself can also create problems. The sense of wildness can be lost when large numbers of tourists gather round to watch the animals. Also the sheer wear and tear of vehicles may damage the environment.

POACHING ▶

Poaching is the name given to the illegal killing of animals from game reserves. Some people do this so that they can sell valuable skins or ivory tusks and horns. The photograph shows the skulls of 205 rhinoceros, which were killed for their horns in Zambia. The theft of large numbers of animals of the same kind affects other animals and changes the natural balance in the area.

MADAGASCAR ▼

Madagascar is one of Africa's special places. Here there are animals that are not found anywhere else in the world, such as lemurs. Yet in this poor country, much of the tropical forest, where many of these animals and plants are found, has been cut down. People have destroyed the forest to grow their food, and they will eventually destroy the landscape altogether. However, the World Wide Fund for Nature is providing money and expertise to help Madagascar preserve its natural treasures.

CHAD

Lake Chad

SUDAN

NIGERIA

CENTRAL AFRICAN REPUBLIC

ADAMAOUA MOUNTAINS

Mount Cameroon (13,353ft/4,070m)

CAMEROON
Douala
Bangui
Yaounde
Malabo

GULF OF GUINEA

EQUATORIAL GUINEA

Libreville

GABON

SÃO TOMÉ AND PRINCIPE

Garamba National Park

Uele

ETHIOPIA

SOMALIA

White Nile

Lake Turkana

UGANDA

Kampala

Odzala National Park

Zaire

Kisangani
Boyoma Falls

Kisumu

KENYA

Mount Kenya (17,058ft/5,200m)

Marsabit Game Reserve

Masai Mara National Park

Congo

ZAIRE

RWANDA
Kigali

Bukavu

Nairobi

Brazzaville

Pointe Noire
CABINDA (Angola)

Kinshasa
Matadi

Bujumbura
BURUNDI

Lake Tanganyika

Serengeti National Park

TANZANIA

Dodoma

Zanzibar
Dar es Salaam

Mombasa

INDIAN OCEAN

Kananga
Mbuji-Maya

Lualaba

Luanda

Kwango

Kasai

Tsaso National Park

ANGOLA

ATLANTIC OCEAN

Lobito

Likasi
Lubumbashi

Lake Bangweula

Njika Plateau National Park

Ruvuma

Moroni

COMOROS

Antseranana

Huambo

Kitwe

Lake Malawi

MALAWI

Moçambique

Porto Alexandre National Park

ZAMBIA

Lusaka

Lilongwe

Cubango

Kafue National Park

Zambezi

Harare

Victoria Falls

Okavango Swamp

ZIMBABWE

Mutare

MOZAMBIQUE CHANNEL

Toamasina

Antananarivo

MADAGASCAR

Namib

NAMIBIA

Beira

Francistown

Windhoek

BOTSWANA

KALAHARI

Limpopo

Tropic of Capricorn

Kalahari Gemsbok National Park

DESERT

Gaborone

Kruger National Park

Pretoria

Johannesburg

Maputo

Mbabane
SWAZILAND

Desert

REPUBLIC OF

Vaal

Welkom

DRAKENSBERG MOUNTAINS

Kimberley
Bloemfontein

Maseru
LESOTHO

Pietermaritzburg
Durban

Orange

SOUTH AFRICA

Addo Elephant National Park

East London

Cape Town
Cape of Good Hope

Port Elizabeth

Castillo de Belliver, 1983

WALVIS BAY (South Africa)

Lake

Equator

SOUTHWEST ASIA

Most of Southwest Asia consists of desert or very dry country. However, along the Mediterranean coast there are rich agricultural lands. This agriculture is only possible through artificial irrigation and it relies on the waters of the region's great rivers. The River Jordan flows into the Red Sea, and the rivers Euphrates and Tigris flow into the Persian Gulf. It was here that people first tilled the soil and built cities, and it is therefore known as the cradle of civilization.

FERTILE CRESCENT ▼

About 10,000 years ago, this region of the world saw drastic changes which had a severe effect on the landscape. A fertile crescent stretches from Jericho (Jordan and Israel), through Syria into Turkey, Iraq and Iran. Here the first experiments in turning wild wheat into cereal crops began. With the chance to grow their own food, sometimes on terraced hillsides (below), people began to settle in larger communities and the first towns and cities grew up.

IRRIGATION ▲

On the fertile banks of the great rivers Euphrates (above) and Tigris, people grew cereals using simple irrigation techniques as long as 7,500 years ago.

WATER WARS

Water wheels like those in the Syrian city of Hama (above right), on the River Orontes have been drawing water to irrigate the land for thousands of years. However, irrigation then, as now, led to soil salination (in which water draws salts to the soil surface by evaporation), making it useless for agriculture. Sometimes this meant that the people living in the ruined area had to move elsewhere in order to find good soil on which to farm. People seem to have been spoiling the environment for future generations for thousands of years.

Water is a very valuable commodity in this region of the world. Several countries share the same rivers. In January 1990, Turkey began filling the huge Ataturk Dam on the Euphrates, cutting the flow of water downstream to Syria. The two countries reached an agreement that more water should reach Syria. Further downstream, Iraq and Syria came close to war because of Syria's Tabaqah Dam on the Euphrates, which was reducing Iraq's water supply. Water may yet become a cause for war in the future.

30°

N
W · E
S

| 0 | | | 500 | | | 1000 | | | 1500 km |

cm 1 2 3 4 5 6 7 8 9 10

inches 1 2 3 4

| 0 | 500 | 1000 miles |

BULGARIA

BLACK SEA

Istanbul
Sea of
Marmara
Bursa
40°
EGEAN
SEA
EECE
Izmir

Ankara ■   Kizil Irmak   Samsun   Trabzon

TURKEY   Sivas

Lake Tuz Kayseri
ANATOLIA

Mount Ararat
(16,945 ft/5,165 m)
Lake
Van

Konya

TAURUS MOUNTAINS

Antalya   Adana

Halab

CYPRUS

Nicosia ■

Tripoli

LEBANON

Beirut ■

Damascus ■

Haifa
Tel Aviv-Yafo   Irbid   Zarqa
Jerusalem ■   **Amman** ■
Gaza   Dead Sea
ISRAEL   JORDAN

SYRIA

Al Mawsil

Kirkuk

IRAQ

MESOPOTAMIA

SYRIAN

DESERT

Euphrates

Bakhtaran

Baghdad ■

Tigris

Khorramshahr
Basra
Abadan

KUWAIT

Kuwait ■

CASPIAN SEA

KURDISTAN

ZAGROS

Araks

Tabriz

Lake
Urmia
Urumiyeh

Rasht

ELBURZ MOUNTAINS

Tehran ■

Qom

Mashhad

DASHT-E-
KAVIR

IRAN

Esfahan

Kerman

Shiraz
Kazerun

MOUNTAINS

THE PERSIAN   GULF

AFGHANISTAN

30°

MEDITERRANEAN
SEA

EGYPT

Gulf of
Aqaba

AN NAFUD

Buraydah

SAUDI
ARABIA

NEJD

HIJAZ

Medina

RED SEA

Tropic of Cancer

Jiddah   Mecca

SUDAN

Dhahran
BAHRAIN   **Al Manamah** ■
Al Hafuf   QATAR   Dubai
Doha ■
Abu Dhabi ■

UNITED ARAB
EMIRATES

Bandar' Abbas
Straits of
Hormuz

OMAN

GULF OF OMAN

Muscat ■

Riyadh ■

OMAN

RUB' AL KHALI

Salalah

HADHRAMAUT

20°

ARABIAN
SEA

San'a ■   YEMEN

Al Hudaydah   Ta'izz

Mukalla

Aden

Socotra
(Yemen)

DJIBOUTI   GULF OF ADEN

ETHIOPIA

SOMALIA

10°

30°   40°   50°   60°

WAR IN THE GULF

Although there has not been a world war since 1945, wars have been part of the life of many countries since then. Apart from destroying homes and agricultural land, war can have a devastating effect on the environment in general. In the spring of 1991, a war took place in Southwest Asia, which caused a great deal of damage. In August 1990, Iraq had invaded the small but oil-rich country of Kuwait. Most of the rest of the world was incensed by this act of aggression and an alliance was formed to remove the invaders. Eventually, the Iraqis were forced to leave Kuwait in defeat. During this war, destruction of the environment was used as a weapon. Before leaving Kuwait, Iraqi soldiers released more than 3 million barrels of oil from Kuwait's coastal oil refineries into the waters of the Persian Gulf and set fire to its oil wells.

▲ Large numbers of refugees bring many problems.

OIL ON TROUBLED WATERS

During the war with Iraq, Iraqi soldiers dumped oil into the Persian Gulf. The damage from this oil was not as bad as experts first thought. Certain physical features of the Gulf environment probably helped keep the amount of damage caused by the oil in check. In another place, the pollution could have been worse.

The water of the Persian Gulf is very salty, and this means that things float much more easily on the surface. This gives clean-up workers more time to disperse the oil before it sinks to the sea bed. This area is also very hot, and these high temperatures meant that the poisonous chemicals in the oil evaporated quickly, making the oil less harmful to life. In these warm conditions, there is also a much greater chance of the bacteria that consume the oil working quickly to turn it into harmless chemicals.

◀ During the war, many of Kuwait's oil wells were deliberately set alight. The smoke cloud created by so many burning wells turned day into night and caused many pollution problems in the region.

▲ Armies change the face of the desert.

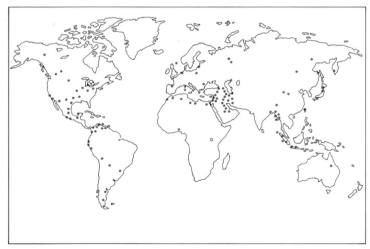

▲ This map shows the most important oil fields of the world.

◀ The oil that was allowed to pour into the Persian Gulf killed an estimated 20,000 birds. These included Great Cormorants, Great Crested Grebes and Black-necked Grebes.

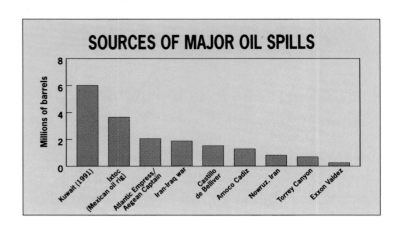

SOURCES OF MAJOR OIL SPILLS

Millions of barrels

Kuwait (1991) · Ixtoc (Mexican oil rig) · Atlantic Empress/ Aegean Captain · Iran-Iraq war · Castillo de Bellver · Amoco Cadiz · Nowruz, Iran · Torrey Canyon · Exxon Valdez

TORCHES IN THE DESERT

Iraqi soldiers also blew up many of Kuwait's precious oil wells. The oil would normally be pumped off and exported to other countries. When the wells began to burn, however, the oil ignited as it came rushing out of the ground, creating blazing torches many meters high. The thick, black smoke spread for some distance, turning day into night. At one stage, the smoke was detected by satellites 1,200km (750 miles) away from the war zone, and black rain fell nearly 1,000km (600 miles) away in Turkey.

However, many of the problems caused by this acrid smoke occurred in the area immediately under the smoke cloud. There is a high level of sulfur in Kuwaiti oil. This means that when water mixes with the smoke from burning wells, it turns into acid rain. There is also the risk that drinking water and soil may be poisoned. Some people living in the area, especially old people and children, have reported breathing problems. At one point during the war, some 650 oil fires were burning in Kuwait. The smoke cloud hung at a level of about 3-4,500m (10-15,000ft). If the wind had carried the cloud to a higher level, it might have affected the climate, changing rainfall patterns in other parts of the world.

◀ This building in Riyadh was destroyed when a Patriot missile landed on it. It is an obvious sign of the destruction that war can bring. Destruction of the environment, however, is sometimes more difficult to see.

MAKING WAR ON THE LAND

The impact of war on the land can take many forms. The sheer number of soldiers that came from other countries caused problems, and thousands of refugees fleeing the war added to this. Each army set up bases in the desert war zone. The waste created by the armies and by the large numbers of refugees created by the war, includes rubbish, poisonous waste and sewage.

Heavy vehicles, such as tanks and helicopters, leave deep ruts in the surface of the desert. These vehicles pack the ground down so that plants cannot grow in the soil. Tank tracks left in the Mojave Desert more than 50 years ago are still there today. Those made in Saudi Arabia, Kuwait and Iraq may take 30-50 years to disappear.

Modern warfare can devastate the environment for people, animals and plants. Chemical weapons such as the herbicides used to defoliate the forests during the Vietnam War (see page 48) were not used during the war in the Gulf. And it seems that the use of nuclear weapons is becoming less probable (see page 52). However, if others follow Iraq's example, and start to use environmental weapons, such as oil and air pollution, the effects could be just as catastrophic.

▲ Army helicopters create a storm of dust.

COMMONWEALTH OF INDEPENDENT STATES

The Commonwealth of Independent States (CIS) is the new name for the former USSR. It is dominated by Russia, the largest country in the world. Its landscapes range from the frozen wastes of Siberia in the north, down to the much warmer parts around the Black Sea and the Caspian Sea. Because it is so large it has vast natural resources in coal, oil, natural gas, and other valuable minerals as well as productive farmland for growing wheat and raising livestock.

NUCLEAR DISASTER ▼

Even with its huge natural sources of energy the CIS uses nuclear power. It was in April 1986 at a nuclear power station at Chernobyl (below), in the Ukraine, that disaster struck. An experiment went wrong and this led to an explosion in the reactor, resulting in a release of radioactivity into the atmosphere. More than 30 people died as a result of the accident and many more are likely to die from diseases such as cancer, which can be caused by radioactivity. In a region 50km (31 miles) southwest of Chernobyl, in the Narodichi district, the levels of radiation were found to be 148 times higher than normal. Much local farmland (below) was contaminated and can no longer be used.

OIL ON THE SNOW ▲

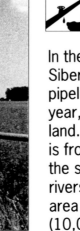

In the oil-rich region of Siberia, about 50 pipelines fracture each year, spilling oil onto the land. Because the ground is frozen, the oil lies on the surface. The land and rivers are polluted. An area of 26,000 sq km (10,000 sq miles) is covered in oil. Ducks and other wildfowl which used to breed in this region, no longer come here. The herds of reindeer have moved away completely. The people in the area are unable to live there any more. Repairs to the 3,000 oil wells in the region are needed, and so are repairs to the 25-year-old pipelines.

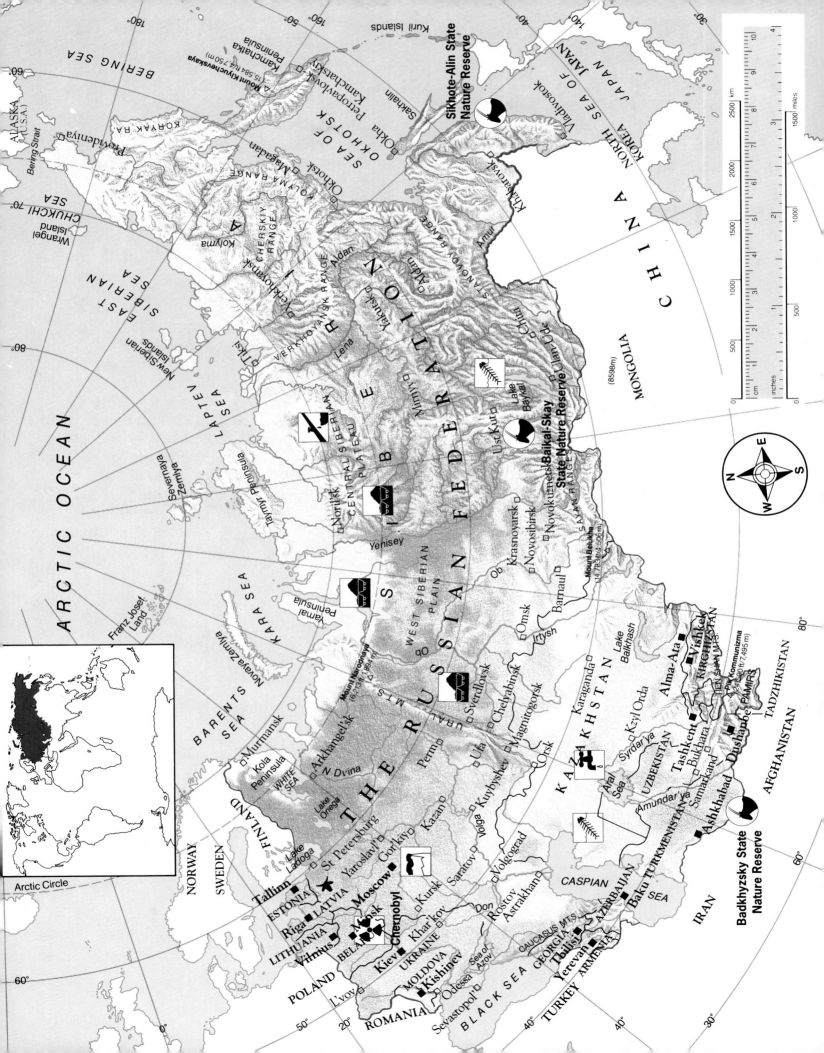

INDIA (and its neighbors)

The Himalayan Mountains link several countries together. Afghanistan, Pakistan, Northern India, Bhutan and Nepal are all mountainous countries. On the western side of the sub-continent is the Thar Desert, which contrasts with the tropical forested areas of Myanmar, which used to be called Burma. Three major rivers, the Indus, Ganges and Brahmaputra, carry the waters of the Himalayas to the lowlands and to the one billion people who live there.

FERTILIZER OR FUEL? ▼

In many parts of the world, people collect animal dung to use as fuel and as a kind of cement for building. Because many forests are disappearing, more people are using dung in this way. The fresh dung is taken from the fields where the animals roam. It is shaped by hand into flat cakes. It is dried in the sun and piled up for later use. Animal dung becomes very hot and burns for a long time, and it does not smell, so it is ideal for cooking.

When mixed with sand and water, it can be used to build low walls, irrigation channels and even the walls of houses. However, if the dung were left on the fields, it would help to fertilise and improve the soil for growing vital food crops.

◀ LIVING WITH TREES

Trees are an essential commodity for rural people all over the world.

They provide fuelwood for cooking and keeping warm. It often falls to the women of a village to collect wood, and if nearby trees are cut down, perhaps to provide charcoal for people living in cities, the women have to walk long distances every day to find other sources of wood.

All over the Indian sub-continent, children are encouraged to replant trees, so that they understand that this resource must be conserved for the future.

TREE HUGGERS ▼

When loggers began to cut down trees close to a village in northern India, the local women wrapped their arms around the trees to save them. Their protest was successful and it grew into a number of similar movements. Their trees were saved and the health of the environment assured.

DEFORESTATION AND SOIL EROSION

The destruction of forests (deforestation) creates more problems than just the loss of trees. Forests hold onto soil and also onto water. When the trees go, the soil is washed away and the water causes flooding. These events happen all over the world and not just in this part of Asia.

The Indian sub-continent has the highest and longest mountain chain in the world – the Himalayas. The great rivers of the Indus, Ganges and Brahmaputra all have their source in these young mountains. Melted snow, rain water and tiny particles of rock start their journey from the mountains, making their way downstream towards the sea. Because the Himalayas are young mountains the soil has had less time to collect together and once every 50 years rain flooded the lowlands of Bangladesh.

Terracing is the traditional way of growing crops on hillside soil. The terrace walls hold on to the soil when it rains, stopping it being washed down the hillside.

That was before the forested foothills of the Himalayas were stripped of their trees. Since the 1970s, floods have happened every four years. That is because over the last 40 years, about 40% of the forests have been cut down. In Nepal alone, half of the forests have disappeared. When the trees are gone, there is nothing to hold the soil onto the sloping sides of the mountains, and with each rain storm a little more is washed down. In the monsoon season, when the rain falls long and hard, landslides are common. When this happens the terraced fields on the mountain slopes are washed away, along with whole villages. As much as 75 tons of soil for each hectare of land can be lost each year. When this amount of soil disappears there is little left for the farmers to grow crops to feed their families, and so they may go hungry at certain times of the year. The result of the deforestation in the mountains is severe flooding down on the lowlands. With the flood

▲ This Bangladeshi woman has survived a flood.

▲ The mouth of the great River Ganges.

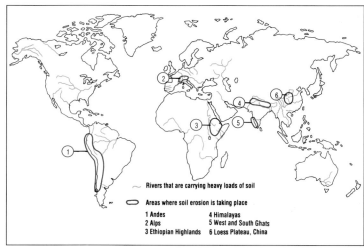

Rivers that are carrying heavy loads of soil

Areas where soil erosion is taking place

1 Andes
2 Alps
3 Ethiopian Highlands
4 Himalayas
5 West and South Ghats
6 Loess Plateau, China

▲ This map shows places where soil is washed into rivers, and rivers that are damaged by this extra soil.

GREEN BHUTAN

In the 1970s the government of Bhutan declared that 60% of the country should always be covered in forest. A rule was made, and nobody was allowed to cut down trees. After this, a tree-planting scheme was introduced and the number of goats was cut back. Bhutan is now the last green patch in the whole of the Himalayas.

▶ An avalanche of soil from above has torn down the trees below, speeding the whole process of deforestation and erosion along.

water comes a vast amount of silt which builds up in the mouths of rivers such as the Ganges. In Bangladesh, millions of people live on tiny islands made from the silt brought down from the Himalayas.

These tiny islands, known as chars, are good for growing crops, because the new soil is very fertile. In some places the islands are no more than a few feet above the water level. When the water level rises

◀ The effects of soil being washed away can be seen on this hillside. There is nothing left except bare rock, and very little lives here.

▲ Rain waters bring fertile soil to the lowlands.

during the monsoon season, or when powerful cyclone winds blow sea waves inland, the people can be washed away. Sometimes the islands themselves are washed away too. This is what happened in Bangladesh in the monsoon of 1991.

Land is in short supply in this region, and the people take the risk of farming in this dangerous area because there is not enough safe farmland to go around.

OPERATION TIGER

Operation Tiger is a conservation success. It was launched by the World Wide Fund for Nature in 1972 to save the tiger, whose numbers had fallen in India from 40,000 in 1930 to less than 2,000 in 1970. The Indian government created tiger reserves all over India and today there are 17 reserves covering 30,000 square kilometers (7.5 million acres). Other countries have followed suit, including Bangladesh, Nepal and Bhutan.

CHINA AND JAPAN (and their neighbors)

China is the third largest country in the world. It includes parts of the Himalayas and the mountains of Tibet, the Gobi desert and plains of Mongolia, and the forested region in the southeast of the country. Japan, on the other hand, is made up of four large islands and about 3,000 smaller ones. It lies in a position where movements in the Earth's crust happen frequently. These can cause earthquakes. Over 60 of Japan's 150 major volcanoes are active.

CHINA'S RICE BOWL ▶

China is a very large country – over 1 billion people live there. In the capital, Beijing (Peking) there are 9 million people. All these people depend on China's "rice bowl," a plateau of land made up of fertile soil called loess. But China's rice bowl is under threat from soil erosion. The loess soils are blown down onto the plains from the surrounding deserts and mountains. Bad farming methods has meant that much of this valuable soil is washed into the Yellow River.

ONE-CHILD FAMILIES ▲▶

China and Japan both suffer from over-population. In China, the government has tried to solve this problem by telling couples that they can have only one child each. In this way, it is hoped that future generations will shrink in numbers. The poster (right) uses symbols and words to tell people that a one-child family is a prosperous family.

NATURAL DISASTER ▶

Some places are especially at risk from earthquakes and erupting volcanoes. This is because the Earth's surface (the crust and upper mantle) is split into several sections, or plates. These lie on top of a semi-molten layer of liquid rock in the upper

mantle. Movements in this layer shift the plates around, and earthquakes occur. Volcanoes are places where the liquid rock is forced out, onto the surface. Japan lies on a plate that is sliding underneath another, so earthquakes are quite common. From 1960 to 1981, there were 43 earthquakes and other natural disasters in this region.

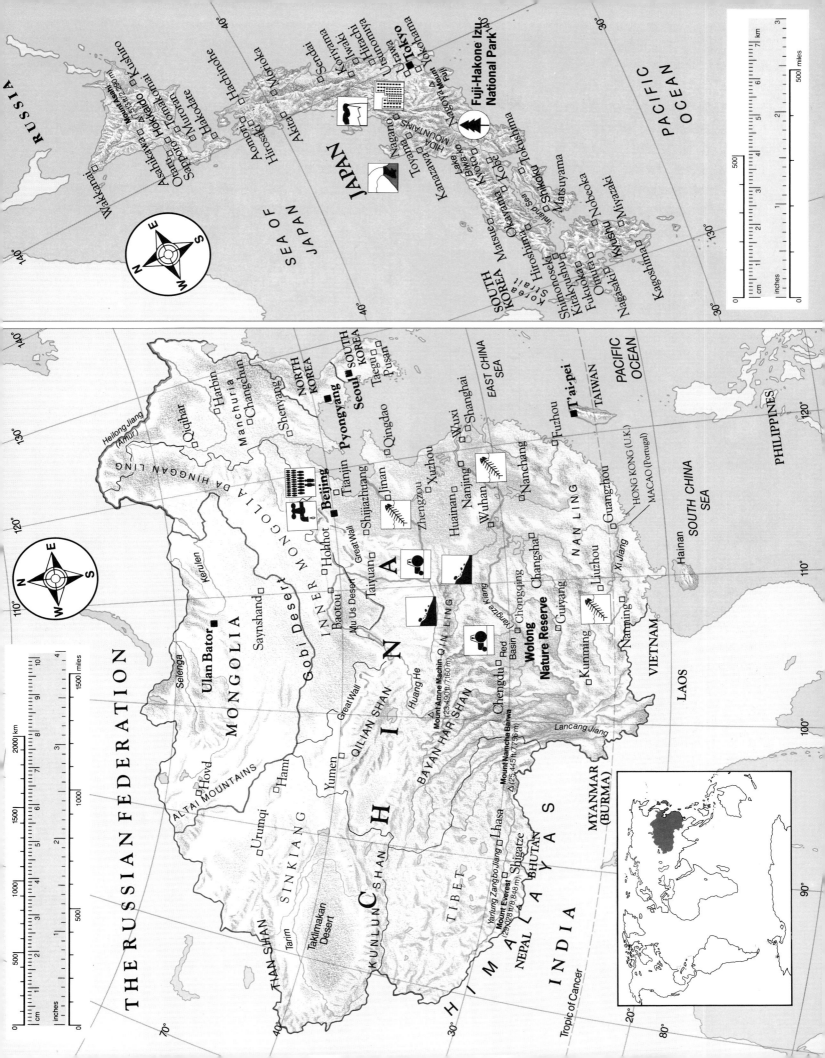

SOUTHEAST ASIA

Much of Southeast Asia is made up of thousands of islands. Each has its own kinds of features, such as mountains and caves, and there are many beautiful coral reefs along the coasts. The islands all have some kind of tropical forest.

Much of the forest has been cut down, and what little remains is being rapidly removed. Unfortunately, large areas of Southeast Asia have recently been subject to wars, and the landscape and inhabitants have all suffered as a result.

CLAMS AND MICA ▲

In Irian Jaya, there are plans to mine the Wandamen mountains for mica, a kind of rock. This is used in metallic car paint and some cosmetics. If the plans go ahead, the mica dust will get into the local rivers, and then into the marine nature reserve, Teluk Cenderawasih. The dust will blanket the coral reef and clog up the breathing and feeding mechanisms of the giant clams (above) that live there. The clams and the reef provide food for 10,000 people in the area and will be at risk if the mine opens.

DEFORESTATION ▶

Since the Vietnam War, huge areas of tropical forest in Southeast Asia have been stripped to supply other countries with wood for furniture. This deforestation causes major changes in the environment. In north-western Peninsular Malaysia, the disappearance of the forest has meant that the amount of rain falling in the region has been reduced. This has stopped the growing of rice in wet fields (called paddies). In all, 20,000 hectares (50,000 acres) of paddy fields have been abandoned.

THE VIETNAM WAR ▼

During the Vietnam War (in the 1960s), millions of liters of herbicides were sprayed onto the forests of southern Vietnam, destroying them. This was done so that enemy soldiers could be more easily seen among the trees. Because of soil erosion, chemical warfare and farming, Vietnam's forests have now almost disappeared.

AUSTRALIA AND NEW ZEALAND

Australia is a large continent, made up mostly of desert. The whole of the middle of the island is completely dry for much of the year. Around the east coast, the climate is much less dry, and this is where most of the people live. In the north there are tropical forests. Tasmania is different. Large forests cover this smaller island, and the climate is very wet and cool. New Zealand's South Island has spectacular fiords, similar to those of Norway.

◀REEF IN DANGER

The crown of thorns starfish was once thought to be quite rare. Then, in 1963 swarms were reported on the Great Barrier Reef, to the north of Australia. This starfish feeds on coral polyps, the living animals that are found inside hard coral. Once the coral dies, the skeleton of the reef grows over with a layer of algae, which is ideal for the starfish to lay its eggs in. When the starfish move in, however, the fish and other animals of the reef leave altogether. Huge areas of the Great Barrier Reef have been eaten away by the crown of thorns starfish, and the destruction continues to this day. Nobody is sure what caused the population explosion during the 1960s, but scientists are now working on ways to control the starfish, and perhaps ensure that this beautiful reef and its other inhabitants survive.

DRY LAND ▲

Deserts cover about a third of Australia, and droughts affect 55% of the land area. Eastern Australia, which normally has enough rain for farming, suffered a drought in 1982-3. Some scientists thought that the Peruvian current El Nino may have caused it, together with droughts in other parts of the world. In Australia, the land is also overgrazed, causing soil erosion. In parts of the drier regions, irrigation causes salts in the soil to be brought to the surface, making it too salty to grow crops.

TASMANIA'S FORESTS▲

The temperate forests of Tasmania saw a strange battle for their survival when, in the early 1980s, hundreds of protesters blocked the way of loggers who wanted to cut down a unique forest

landscape. Forest of this kind is found nowhere else in the world, yet the loggers had been given permission to cut it down. Because of the protest, the government of Australia decided that the Tasmanian forests should be saved, and this unique place is now a World Heritage Area.

THE PACIFIC ISLANDS

The Pacific Ocean covers almost half the Earth and it has thousands of small islands. Some of these islands are the peaks of volcanoes which have their base on the ocean bed. Hawaii has two peaks which emerge 4,200m (13,780ft) out of the sea, and are under the sea to a depth of 6,000m (19,685ft). There are three different kinds of islands: the continental islands, which are connected to the mainland under the sea; volcanic islands; and coral islands.

NUCLEAR TESTING ▶

Some of the islands of the Pacific have been used to test nuclear weapons. The photograph shows an explosion on Bikini Atoll in 1946. On exploding, the bombs give off radiation into the atmosphere and produce the poisonous element strontium-90. Since the testing in the Pacific, this has been found in the bodies of animals and people as far away as the Arctic. A partial ban on exploding nuclear bombs into the atmosphere was signed in 1963, and by 1980 the last test was carried out in China, although France continues to test underground.

Nuclear war would have a devastating effect on the world. Apart from the effects of radiation, dust would enter the atmosphere and block out the Sun. During this "nuclear winter," the climate would change and nothing could grow.

ISLAND BUILDING ▼

Many of the Pacific islands are made by volcanic eruptions. Eventually, the bare rock of the volcano is colonized by plants, particularly the coconut, whose seeds float across the sea. Animals are transported here by wind and ocean currents. Often, a coral reef grows in the warm sea around the island. Sometimes the volcanic rock of the island sinks back into the sea, leaving the coral that has built up to form a coral island, or atoll, surrounding a central body of water, called a lagoon.

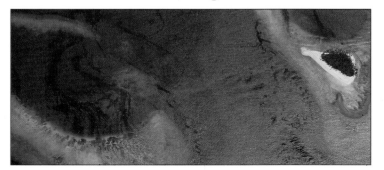

TYPHOON WARNING ▲

Many of the islands in this region are not much higher than the level of the sea itself. As a result, they are in danger from the effects of typhoons, flooding and other natural disasters, which can happen without much warning. Typhoons are storms which occur over warm tropical oceans. They spin faster and faster, and the winds blow at up to 200km (125 miles) per hour. The photograph shows the results of Typhoon Roy, in January 1988, on the island of Guam.

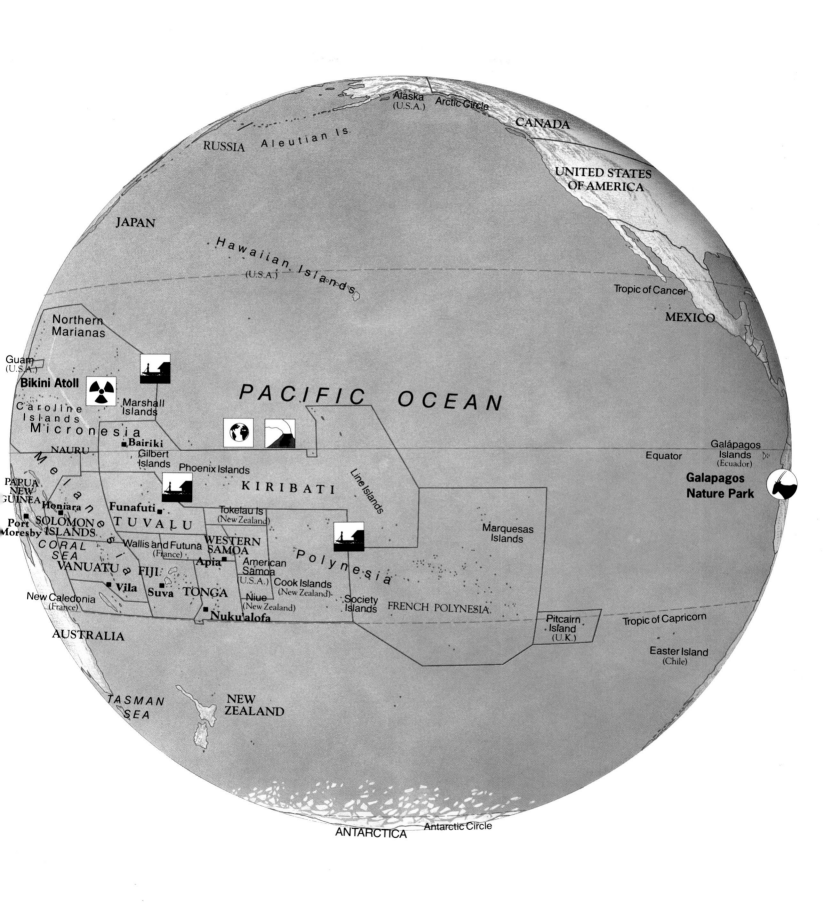

RUSSIA Aleutian Is.

Alaska
(U.S.A.) Arctic Circle CANADA

UNITED STATES
OF AMERICA

JAPAN

Hawaiian Islands
(U.S.A.)

Tropic of Cancer

MEXICO

PACIFIC OCEAN

Northern
Marianas

Guam
(U.S.A.)

Bikini Atoll

Caroline
Islands
Micronesia

Marshall
Islands

NAURU

Bairiki
Gilbert
Islands

Galápagos
Islands
(Ecuador)

Equator

Galapagos
Nature Park

Phoenix Islands

Melanesia

KIRIBATI

Line Islands

PAPUA
NEW
GUINEA

Honiara

Funafuti

Tokelau Is
(New Zealand)

Marquesas
Islands

Port
Moresby

SOLOMON
ISLANDS

TUVALU

WESTERN
SAMOA

Polynesia

CORAL
SEA

Wallis and Futuna
(France)

Apia

American
Samoa
(U.S.A.)

Cook Islands
(New Zealand)

VANUATU

FIJI

Vila

Suva

TONGA

Niue
(New Zealand)

Society
Islands

FRENCH POLYNESIA

New Caledonia
(France)

Nuku'alofa

Pitcairn
Island
(U.K.)

Tropic of Capricorn

AUSTRALIA

Easter Island
(Chile)

TASMAN
SEA

NEW
ZEALAND

ANTARCTICA Antarctic Circle

GLOBAL WARMING

Many of the Pacific's coral islands lie no more than 2-3m (6.5-10ft) above sea level, and so are at risk from flooding when natural disasters such as typhoons occur. However, there is another threat to these islands, and to other low-lying regions. This threat is the risk of rising water levels caused by the greenhouse effect and global warming.

THE GREENHOUSE EFFECT
Some of the heat that reaches us from the Sun is trapped inside the gaseous envelope of the atmosphere, like an enormous greenhouse. This is known as the greenhouse effect, and without it, the Sun's heat would be lost to space, and the Earth would be too cold to support life. The gases that trap heat from the Sun include carbon dioxide. Problems

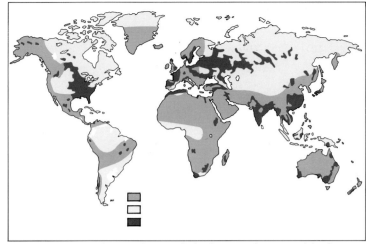
▲ This map shows how global warming could change the world's rainfall pattern.

arise when the amount of carbon dioxide and other gases in the atmosphere increases, raising the temperature of the Earth.

In the early 1800s, the level of carbon dioxide in the air was 280 parts per million. In the 1990s, the amount of carbon dioxide has risen to 350 parts per million, and is still rising. Four-fifths of this extra carbon dioxide comes from burning fossil fuels, such as coal and oil and petrol. The rest comes from burning trees, especially in the tropical rainforests. Although carbon dioxide is to blame for about half the warming that scientists have detected in the climate, chlorofluorocarbons (CFCs) contribute another quarter. The rest is caused by natural gases, such as methane from growing rice.

▲ Power stations and industry add to global warming.

RISING SEA LEVELS
When water warms up, it expands. This combines with extra water in the seas from melting polar ice caps. When the water level rises, it threatens to flood

▲ Rising water levels may flood areas like Bangladesh.

▲ The Thames barrier protects London from high tides.

low-lying regions. Over the next century the sea could rise by a meter (3ft) or more. Although the water will not completely cover all the islands, it will increase the chances of flooding at high tide or during high winds. Flooding with sea water will also mean that freshwater supplies on land will be spoiled by salty sea water. Coral reefs around islands act as a barrier, protecting them from large waves. If the water level rises, the reefs will lie lower in the water, and their protection is lost.

There are many other areas that will be affected by global warming and the rise in sea level. In Bangladesh, 18% of the land would disappear under water, making 17 million people homeless. The Thames barrier would offer little protection to London. Manhattan island, in New York, stands only 1.2m (4ft) above sea level, and so it, too, is at risk.

CHANGING CLIMATE PATTERNS

When the Earth's temperature rises, it also changes climate patterns. Areas that are now used to heavy rainfall will probably become drier. This would mean

COUNTRIES ADDING CARBON TO THE ATMOSPHERE BY BURNING FOSSIL FUELS (in millions of tons)		
	1960s	1980s
United States	791	1224
CIS (former USSR)	396	1035
China	215	594
United Kingdom	161	156
Poland	55	128
India	33	151

that places such as the Midwest of the USA, which grow a lot of the world's grain, may become drier, and the amount of grain produced will fall. Regions that are already dry, such as the Sahel region in Africa, may experience worse droughts than before.

It is essential that we slow down the rate of global warming. This can only be done by cutting back the burning of fossil fuels, conserving energy, stopping the removal of trees, and replanting more trees to absorb the extra carbon dioxide in the atmosphere.

▲ Traffic pollution increases carbon dioxide levels.

▲ Pacific islands are at risk from rising water levels.

THE GALAPAGOS ISLANDS NATIONAL PARK

These stark volcanic islands lie off the coast of Ecuador. The islands are home to a unique selection of animals, including giant tortoises, large iguana lizards and several different species of fish. It was here that Charles Darwin made observations on the island's wildlife that were later to help him formulate his theory of evolution. Even though it is a national park, the natural habitat has been put in danger by the introduction of goats, which have eaten the vegetation.

The Arctic is not a landmass, but an ocean surrounded by the land of several different countries. The North Pole is actually a piece of permanent pack ice. Within the Arctic Circle there are parts of Canada, Alaska (which belongs to the USA), Scandinavia and the USSR. In this area is the tundra, a region that covers 15% of the Earth's surface. It is an area of frozen earth and few inhabitants. Only the top 50cm (20in) of snow thaws, and then for just three months of every year.

OZONE HOLE ▶

Both the Arctic and the Antarctic have played their part in increasing our understanding of a major danger to the health of the whole world. This danger is the hole in the ozone layer.

The ozone layer is a thin envelope of the gas ozone, which surrounds the Earth at a height of 20-25km (12.5-15.5 miles). This layer helps to protect the Earth's surface from the Sun's ultraviolet rays. Although some of these rays reach the Earth, too many would be harmful to the health of all living things.

The ozone layer is essential for the survival of all life on Earth, yet over the last 20 years, scientists have found that the amount of ozone is decreasing. The first evidence of this came when a British team of scientists in the Antarctic noticed that there was no ozone in the atmosphere above the region they were studying. In January 1989 scientists studying the ozone layer above the Arctic found a similar, smaller, hole there.

▲ South of the Arctic ice lies a region of tundra.

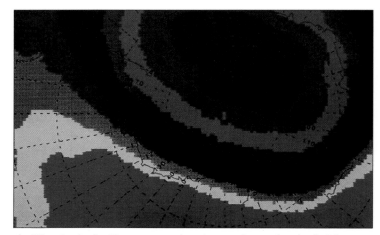

▲ The hole in the ozone is shown here in dark blue.

The hole is created by chemicals called chlorofluorocarbons (CFCs). These are used in such products as aerosol sprays, refrigerators and air-conditioning units. Fortunately, there has been an international agreement to phase out the use of CFCs by the year 2000.

ARCTIC SMOG

The North Pole draws air pollution towards it from the industrial countries of the northern hemisphere. In winter, a yellow haze hangs over the area, and poisonous chemicals have been found in the ice and in Arctic animals.

▲ The Arctic is covered with snow all year round.

THE ANTARCTIC

The Antarctic is almost completely covered in snow and ice. The ice is nearly 4.5km (almost 3 miles) thick in places. Underneath this white landscape, however, there lies an unseen land. Here is one of the world's longest mountain chains – the Transantarctic Mountains. Antarctica is also the highest continent in the world. On average, it is three times higher than the other continents. The highest mountain is Vinson Massif at 4,900m (16,000ft).

WHITE WILDERNESS ▶

Antarctica is the last untouched wilderness on Earth. Because there is so much snow and ice, very few plants and animals live there. Some animals, such as seals and penguins, stop there for a short time to breed. The only living things that can survive Antarctica all year round are a few tiny insects and some types of moss. In recent years, tourists have become interested in visiting this white wilderness. This environment is so fragile that even small numbers of people could cause great harm.

▲ *Scientific research stations study every aspect of the continent.*

MINERAL WEALTH

Many different minerals have been found in Antarctica. These include coal in the Transantarctic Mountains, iron ore in the Prince Charles Mountains and oil under the sea.

In 1957 and 1958 there was an agreement between some 12 countries that they would only use Antarctica for peaceful purposes. This agreement was called the Antarctic Treaty, and it meant that the Antarctic could only be used for scientific research. However, in 1988, the same countries decided to exploit the continent for its minerals.

Two countries, Australia and France, realized the danger the continent was in and they asked for it to be declared an International Wilderness reserve. In 1991, 39 nations agreed that there should be no mining here for another 50 years.

As long as most countries agree that Antarctica should not be exploited, the continent is safe. The problem will come when world resources begin to run out, and people look to Antarctica for their minerals.

The hope is that everyone will agree that Antarctica should be a protected area that nobody can destroy.

▲ *Tourism is a growing threat to Antarctica's safety.*

GLOSSARY AND FURTHER INFORMATION

Here are simple explanations of some of the main terms used throughout the book.

Balance of Nature A state of balance between all living things, including people, animals and plantlife.

Conservation The protection and management of the natural world.

Environment The surroundings and circumstances – type of land, climate, other animals and plants and so on – that an animal or plant lives in.

Fossil Fuels Includes fuels such as coal from plants and oil from the bodies of fossilized animals, and the gas that is given off by them (natural gas). As fossil fuels burn, they give off carbon dioxide, which adds to global warming.

Habitat A specific kind of area where a particular animal or plant naturally lives or grows.

Habitat Destruction The destruction of natural habitats by people. The habitat changes so the animals and plants living there no longer have a natural home.

Hunting When one animal kills another for food. When people hunt animals, it is often not just for food. It can be for the skin of an animal, for sport, a living animal for research, or for the pet trade.

Intensive Agriculture Farming by using unnatural methods for growing crops, such as artificial fertilizers or insecticides for killing pests. Such practices increase the amount of food produced, but risk damaging the natural systems of the environment.

Irrigation The watering of the land by artificial means so that crops can be grown in otherwise dry areas. When poor methods are used, this leads to salination of the soil.

National Park An officially protected place where the environment can be looked after without it being changed or damaged by people. In most national parks, people are welcome, and may actually be a part of the way the park works.

Nature/Game Reserve An area where animals and plants are protected from disturbance by people.

Ozone Layer A layer of ozone gas in the atmosphere, which blocks out the harmful ultraviolet rays of the sun.

Pollution The process of putting poisonous substances into the environment. For example getting rid of chemicals produced by industry by putting them into rivers.

Typhoons, Hurricanes and Cyclones These are all names given to tropical storms. Typhoons are storms happening over the Pacific Ocean, cyclones are storms over the Indian Ocean and hurricanes are storms over the Atlantic Ocean.

UNEP (United Nations Environment Programme) A United Nations program, set up to guide and co-ordinate the repair of the damage done to our environment, and prevent further degradation, in a global effort to save our planet. The UNEP is currently working to help clean up the Mediterranean.

FURTHER INFORMATION

Here is a selection of organizations in the United States and Canada which are actively involved in helping to protect animals all over the world.

You can write to these organizations for further information.

The Sierra Club
730 Polk Street
San Francisco, CA 94109

Friends of the Earth
218 D Street S.E.
Washington, DC 20077-0936
 also
251 Laurier Avenue West,
Suite 701
Ottawa, Ontario K1P 5J6

Greenpeace
1436 U Street N.W.
P.O. Box 3720
Washington, DC 20007
 also
185 Spadina Avenue
Toronto, Ontario M5T 2C6

National Audubon Society
950 3rd Avenue
New York, NY 10022

Earth Island Institute
301 Broadway
San Francisco, CA 94133

Environmental Defense Fund
257 Park Avenue South
New York, NY 10010

The Wilderness Society
1400 Eye Street N.W.
Washington, DC 20005

Conservation International
1015 18th Street N.W.,
Suite 1000
Washington, DC 20036

Save the Rainforest/
Rainforest Action Network
301 Broadway, Suite A
San Francisco, CA 94133

The Rainforest Alliance
295 Madison Avenue
Suite 1804
New York, NY 10017

MAP INDEX

63

INDEX OF PLACES AND THREATS TO THE ENVIRONMENT

FRANKLIN PIERCE COLLEGE LIBRARY

00084820

DATE DUE

JUL 3 0 '95		
JUN 1 3 '98		
APR 0 7 '99		
DEC 0 3 2003		
JAN 0 2 2008		
GAYLORD		PRINTED IN U.S.A.